TWO HUNDRED MILES FROM BAGHDAD

By The Same Author

Violence, Veils and Bloodlines -- Reporting from War Zones

Thoreau, The Kid and Mr. Lou -- Book Notes of a Foreign Correspondent

Some of the stories in this book are in the author's earlier writings, though in totally different contexts.

Published by Piscataqua Press
Portsmouth, NH

ISBN: 9781958669303

TWO HUNDRED MILES FROM BAGHDAD

BY LOUIS J. SALOME

The author invites readers to send their most unusual and interesting hitchhiking stories to the following email address: hitchingatwill@gmail.com

Please include your name and the year and context of each story.

Thank you, Lou Salome

For my wife, Patricia Brothers Salome,

without whose love and support our adventurous

life would not have been possible.

CONTENTS

FOREWORD

Hitchhiking hit the road with the automobile and a penniless person sticking a thumb out and swinging an arm back and forth. So it's been reported. During hard times, young men bumming with no prospects — and thumbs in — took a bigger risk and leaped on rolling railroad cars. Unrecorded are the countless others who for eons bummed rides on stallions, donkeys, camels, coaches and wagons heading into or out of tents and towns. A good guess is that as long as there have been humans and ways to get around faster than using their own two legs people hitched, in one form or another. Neither Herodotus nor Thucydides pinpointed such historic minutiae, but that doesn't mean they didn't happen.

My hitching life began in knee jerk fashion during high school in the mid-1950s. In my first two years of college, hitching became a daily exercise. After decades of stitching together a career as a newspaperman, I took to hitching again, this time by rail, air, boat, an occasional camel or donkey, as well as by the internal combustion engine. Hitching became my ticket to breaking barriers and gathering news in sometimes dangerous and always fascinating places. At the young but advancing age of sixty-three, lodged in a cabin in the New Hampshire woods writing a book about global tribalism, I hitched again. My goal was to find out how much things had changed after my fifty years on the road. Soon enough I learned to mourn the loss.

Through a mix of awe and disbelief, younger generations laugh when I tell stories about hitching to college in the late

1950s. When an old classmate asked recently what I was working on, a book about hitchhiking, I answered.

"Oh, yeah," my friend remarked with the easy nonchalance of a youthful triumph brought back to life, "I hitched to JFK's inauguration." That was in 1961, our junior year of college. I was not yet twenty.

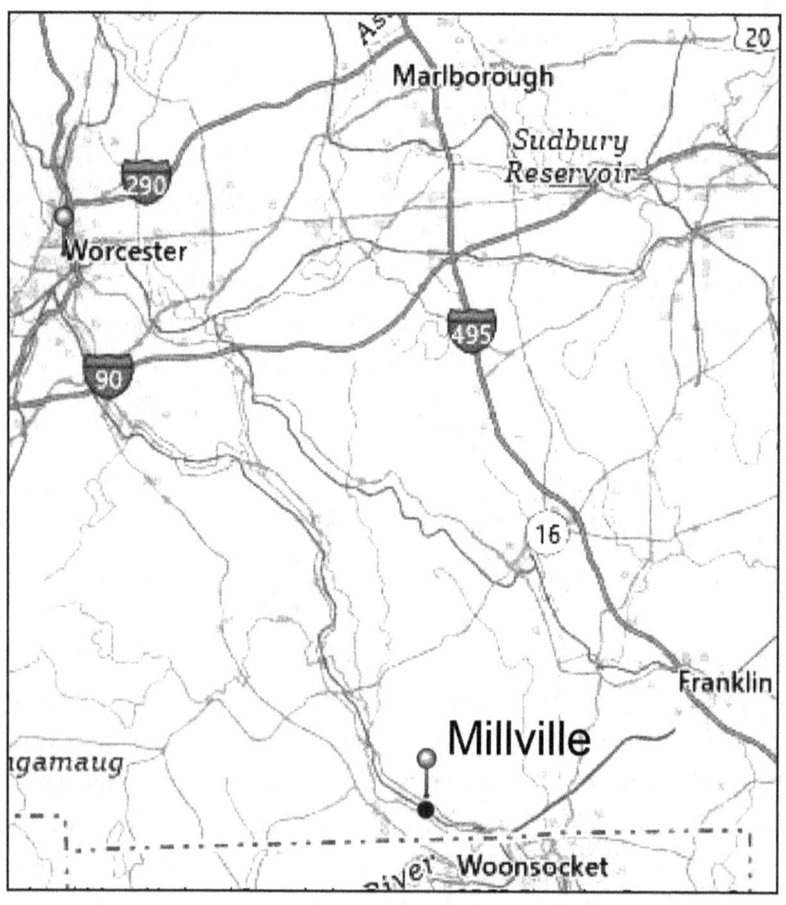

1 | THE ROAD FROM BARNEY'S

Dickie sat on the accelerator and we sped north by northwest from the rising sun. A young man in his prime, Dickie McCrohan was late to work up the line. A hitchhiker, I was on the first leg of a longer journey to college and three more continents. Dickie, only eight years older than I, never seemed to have a down moment. Quick of mind and tongue and bursting with good blarney, it was no surprise that he became one of the best bartenders in the region. Dickie talked non-stop, about anything. The double he hit to win the softball game the night before, dogs in heat, his sexual exploits, but never about wise old Skinchy's ribald riposte that he had more sex by accident than Dickie had on purpose. A town storyteller, Skinchy was much older than Dickie, so no one, not even Dickie, challenged the wise man's prowess.

My college days began in Millville's town center. There, the town's singular flashing amber traffic light matched the pale sun waking over the horizon and hours later lit the town after the heavenly orb took its nightly nap. That blinking amber light marked the daily dawn and dusk of my first two years of college. It was my hitching post outbound and my depot inbound.

Short is one way to describe the drive from Millville to Uxbridge on state road 122 in southeastern Massachusetts. But the spin along the two-lane strip wasn't always too short to be exciting. Halfway between Millville and Uxbridge one mild morning Dickie screeched to a halt for a reason I didn't immediately grasp. Off to the left, well beyond the swale, Dickie had spotted two dogs locked in what seemed to be eternal copulation. The usual key to unlocking that mating ritual, Dickie proclaimed, was to drench the hounds with cold water. I was still too young to know much of the mating ritual of wild dogs, or the primeval tools of decopulation. On that day, neither a tap nor a river was close enough to douse the fire of canine passion. So Dickie tried a more primal solution: he shouted and danced in a circle around the dogs in a weird ritual that I have seen neither before nor since. His valiant five-minute effort to save the species failed. "Let's go, Dickie," I shouted with little sympathy for the mad dogs, "my Uxbridge connection is waiting. We can check on the outcome tomorrow."

"Tomorrow may be too late," answered Dickie, as we drove off.

Friends used to joke that I'd have better luck if I hitched with a lovely lass at my hip. (Come to think of it, no woman at the wheel ever plucked me from the verge: their mistake, not mine.) But I could never convince a friendly female to rise before dawn to join me on the road. I had zero chance of finding a coed to hitch home with me at night because all of my classmates were male. My morning problems were easily solved. As long as I reached Millville's town center by 7:15 a.m., I was assured of a ride with Dickie or Mr. Berkowitz, whoever reached the corner first. Almost like booking a taxi, or an Uber or Lyft today, Dickie or Mr. Berkowitz was there for me. Though I don't recall his first name and maybe never knew it, Mr. Berkowitz and I knew each other the way younger and older people know each other in small towns. We vouched for each other, and our families. Mr. Berkowitz was the strong, silent type. During our seven-mile drive to Uxbridge our conversation never taxed our vocabularies. "Good morning" said it all.

"Good morning, Mr. Berkowitz," I'd say, jumping from the curb into the passenger seat and slamming the car door behind me.

"Yup!" Mr. Berkowitz would say.

"Good day to go to work," I'd say, stupidly.

"Yup!" Mr. Berkowitz would reply.

"How'd the Red Sox do yesterday," I'd blubber, referring to New England's big league baseball club, foolishly still trying to get beyond yup.

"Yup," answered Mr. Berkowitz. He was probably going to work in a mill. At seventeen I was off to Logic 101. Neither of us complained.

Only later did I realize that Dickie and Mr. Berkowitz were cut from opposite ends of the same cloth, reflecting Millville's and humanity's dual personalities. Dickie was the glossy side that always wanted to be heard. Mr. Berkowitz seemed happy within himself, content to just show up. Other teachers filled the gap.

When "tomorrow" arrived, Dickie didn't reach Millville's blinking amber light first, so I rode shotgun with Mr. Berkowitz. The afflicted hounds, by this time husband and wife for sure, had vanished. I was certain that Dickie's dance had rescued the species after all. But I said nothing to Mr. Berkowitz about the previous day's canine mating dance or of Dickie's weird rescue antics.

The time was early September of 1958, the beginning of my first semester in adult school. North Main Street in Uxbridge was my first stop on the road to Holy Cross College in Worcester. In Uxbridge I parachuted from Dickie's or Mr. Berkowitz's car into Danny and Bob's living room. Danny, Bob, or their mother, in no particular order, welcomed me into their living room, or parlor, as we called it then. Lucky for me the brothers DeYoung possessed a car, an early-fifties Chevrolet, and we shared the same destination. Danny drove, and he drove hard, faster even than Dickie when Dickie was late for work. Danny propelled his Chevy to Rene's house a couple of miles north and a slight swerve off Route 122. From there, we roared on, along Route 122 or its variants, through villages and towns named Whitinsville, Northbridge, and Millbury, all the way to our 8:30 classes at Holy Cross, which sat on a hill overlooking gritty Worcester. Along the way, Danny avoided wild dogs and children. Not once in two years was Danny nabbed for speeding, and we never were late for class.

Free of frost heaves that would have raised fault lines in the asphalt, the two-lane path was smooth and wide enough. Cheerless, Route 122 was neither beautiful nor ugly. Few drove south from Uxbridge to Millville, unless armed for baseball or softball games. Conditions always spelled light early morning traffic. A few houses lined the road, closer to Uxbridge, as suburban sprawl was yet unborn. By comparison with Millville, Uxbridge was a bustling town of many large mills, some of which clothed soldiers in World War II.

Hitchhiking was common back in 1958, and I was very much a commoner. Millville and its lone blinking light shadowed me and roughly 1,400 other residents. The town shared a border in southeastern Massachusetts with Rhode Island, once aptly named Rogues Island, a state that's never strayed far from its roots. Hopes high and right thumb pointing north and later south daily, I counted myself as one of the lucky lads in town. Hitching to class was my goal each morning. Destiny and desire would later find me thumbing into and out of war zones in Iraq, Somalia, Kosovo, Bosnia and countries with even more vowels in their names.

During my first year in college, I walked down Lincoln Street past what had been, until a few months before, Barney's blazing bellows a few yards from the flashing signal. Gruff and silent, Barney the Smithy had been a blacksmith who shod horses. At the age of 72, a year and seven months before I began hitching to college, Barney died. He fell while boarding a bus in Woonsocket, Rhode Island, five miles from his barn. That injury, along with "general arteriosclerosis," doomed Barney. In a way, modern transportation, not a kick from an ornery horse, killed Barney, who on his worse days I'd seen flying across the barn, courtesy of an angry nag. Way back then, when I was in high school or grammar school, hay and his thick leather apron saved Barney from serious injury.

All this was a moment in time. Only later did I realize that three eras were flashing by: Barney and his dimming trade were gone; my college ambition lay ahead, along with a career and a longer than anticipated life as a hitchhiker in Africa, Asia and Europe. In my sophomore year, our family moved less than a mile across town. That relocation required a longer dash down Hope Street to Central each morning and back home each night. There was then and remains, fortunately, a bridge over the raging Blackstone River. The forty-eight-mile-long Blackstone River drains fewer than 600 square miles, slightly less than the Missouri/Mississippi River basin's 1.85 million square miles.

A town with a huge and once-humming mill, Millville's good economic times were mostly a memory, like its covered bridge. The number of bars, six, matched the number of churches, which might be called a draw between the elbow-benders and the knee-benders, although the sides, like rye and ginger followed by a cold beer, mixed well. Millville had a long and bumpy birth that stretched across centuries. Along with adjacent Blackstone, Millville was at the beginning part of adjacent Mendon. When Blackstone bolted from Mendon in 1845, the neighborhood called Millville went along, but not forever. Back in 1916, Millville split from Blackstone in a huff over sidewalks. Wars have been fought over lesser issues than lines in cement.

Each day for two years I left Millville farther and farther behind, a much greater distance than the fifty-mile round-trip to and from college. That's no knock on Millville; it's simply the way things turned out. Millville was a great town to call home in the forties and fifties. Despite its economic slide, Millville's vitality and character came from its people and their nicknames. There was Inchy (a large man), wise old Skinchy, and Day Day, a puzzle I never solved; Yee and Yeeca (two names for the same person), Ditz, Pie and Shitty Smitty (a pool room compliment); Midge, Rabbit and Nuckie, all members of the same family, just to crack the dictionary.

No one ran the bases with more joy and speed than Chicken Dean, his arms flapping and his legs splaying, like a fowl.

Just before I reached Barney's old barn, I passed St. Augustine's Catholic Church, now no longer a church. Across from Barney's establishment on Lincoln Street was Borek's Market, which touched Conway's Funeral Home. Borek's and Conway's were connected as life is to death, though at the time I didn't realize the passing link between groceries and bier. On Main Street, Dean's Package Store, which fronted the blinking amber light, also touched Barney's barn to the rear. Nearby stood Ryan's Spa, a convenience store that sold Moxie soda, nickel candy, great frappes made by Loosh, another great nickname, and concealed a felt-covered card table in a rear room where no woman — except Rosie, a proprietor — ever entered.

Above Ryan's creaked Big Louie's small poolroom, which housed its own gambling table in its own male-only back room. Giacomo's barber shop touched a bar and a small tool making shop, which nearly touched Millville's Town Hall. Nearly everything in Millville's snug center touched everything else.

When I strolled past Barney's shuttered barn on my way to the blinking light, most of the men of Millville were already working or on their way to the textile factories, dye houses or machine shops that stretched north and south along the polluted River Blackstone. Except for the eight teachers at Longfellow Elementary, most of the women stayed home to make lunch for their children who walked home from Longfellow at noon for soup and sandwiches and to listen to radio soap operas, and by the mid-fifties to watch the soaps on their new black and white televisions. Kids from Chestnut Hill, the northern part of town, were bused to school carrying their lunch, which made them the original brown-baggers, a name that boarding students in college called day-hops like me.

The teachers at Longfellow Elementary were well schooled in their arts. Irish to their grands and porters, they taught the fine arts of English, arithmetic, geography, history and a little do-re-mi. When I began my college hitching career, I was only four years removed from Miss Mahoney's home room, which I sorely missed because she always ordered a long seventh-inning stretch on fall afternoons so we could listen to the World Series on her radio brought from home. Miss Mahoney was the principal, the boss. She liked baseball, and our tastes ran stride to stride with hers. As a baseball town, Millville was second to none. Our schools trailed badly, however, in the domains of physics, chemistry and biology.

To reach class by 8:30, my job was to reach the amber light in time for Dickie or Mr. Berkowitz and Danny and Bob to do the rest. The return trip was far less reliable. Sometimes I rode with Danny and Bob back to Uxbridge so I could hitch to Millville. The last leg of that journey was like waiting for the next day's sun to rise because few people drove from Uxbridge to Millville or beyond, although I was never ignored so much that I had to hoof it. Often, I was forced to hitch from Worcester to Millville, about twenty-five miles and through too many small towns. When my last classes were late, sometimes I didn't slog through my home portal until midnight. The walk from Holy Cross's hilltop campus to reach Route 146 was downhill. My best hope was a ride from campus to the highway, where I counted snowflakes, raindrops or drops in the evening dew. There I waited and waited, sometimes with Dave, a classmate who hitched to Milford, and occasionally with Harry, who was headed to Uxbridge. My cursing expanded and improved dramatically as cars whizzed past or never approached. Nearly all cars and trucks on American roads back then were Detroit made. Fords, Chevrolets and other General Motors swingers dominated. Chrysler and Dodge models trailed, while Hudson, Studebaker, Packard and American Motors still had rubber on the road. European cars were racing elsewhere. Toyotas, Hondas and Datsuns were racing in. Automakers and their models weren't my friends or enemies. Only their drivers were.

Seeking shelter from snow, rain, sleet and a few times hail under highway overpasses, Dave and I usually hitched from the college gates to Uxbridge. Our hopes rose when we reached Route 122, which hummed with more traffic and coursed through villages and towns. In Uxbridge, Dave pointed his thumb toward home in Milford while mine automatically flipped toward Millville. I wasn't the only Millville kid in college more than sixty-five years ago, but I was the only one with a well-oiled thumb. Most motorists who stopped rather than just pity me and fly by weren't poets or philosophers.

"Where ya headed?" "Whatcha studying?" "Where's Millville?"

Most people who braked for me were friendly. If they weren't friendly, they were silent. No one asked why I was hitching. They knew the answer. No one asked whether hitching was a bother, large or small. They knew the answer to that, too. Hitching wasn't rollicking fun, but my feet didn't bleed either. College students or not, today's high fliers are astounded to learn that I hitched to college for two years. Back in 1958, no one asked whether I was afraid, tired or angry about my predicament. I was none of those because hitching was my choice. Looking back, my experiences in 1958 were a remote form of hybrid learning without a computer and Zoom. Hitching was, believe it or not, a class unto itself.

Hitching deprived me of dormitory chatter and dining hall food fights, late night conversations, thin and broad, about professors, classes, and life. A brown bagger's existence taught other lessons in a different classroom. The dayroom, as the room for day students was called, was small. Scattered in the middle were several card games, poker or pitch, between classes and throughout each day. My abiding image of the dayroom is of large tables pushed together and blanketed with enough greenbacks to make it appear there was no wood and the cash floated in mid-air with nothing to prop it up. Another image is of a fire started in a waste paper basket that leaped to a window curtain, soared and for a moment scared the hell out of the arsonist who lit the blaze because it seemed poised to kiss the dayroom *sayonara*.

Those remembrances are incidentals. Deeply embedded in my memory of college are the numerous philosophy, rhetoric, history and English classes. Whether intended or not, that's where I learned to think critically, to ask questions until I had no more. When a high government official in a Middle East government told me, without intending praise, that I knew too much and asked too many questions, I chuckled to myself because I realized the source of his complaint. Despite the criticism, I knew the critic was wrong because I never knew too much and never asked too many questions.

Another college offered me a full scholarship—room, board, tuition, late night gab sessions, food fights and all the other benefits of campus life. Hitching not required. Instead of accepting what was called a "free ride," I chose to hitch, a different kind of school, to Holy Cross for its reputation and the rigor of its education. My family wasn't poor, but extra money was what other kids had. Family wealth, garnered from bookmaking the ponies, dried up in the early Fifties when Tennessee Sen. Estes Kefauver attacked the gambling syndicates and took police off the bookies' payrolls. Soon after that calamity, my grandfather and family built a restaurant to cushion the fall; the restaurant burned to cinders in an early morning kitchen fire. A hard landing it was, with no insurance. After that shock, we continued to eat well and dress well enough to keep up with friends. When I needed cash for petty college expenses, my grandfather came through.

What I learned most at Holy Cross came from the commonwealth, the collegium—the student body. This became clear long after the fact, as most awareness usually does. I came out of a small high school where most students were more or less the same. Many, if not most, students at Holy Cross were so focused their teeth seemed permanently clenched and their muscled cheeks bulged. Their goals seemed as locked in as their jaws. The enrollment was large enough for the mass to convey intelligence and purpose, and small enough to isolate and learn from individuals. Future artists, doctors, lawyers, dentists, professors, poets, mathematicians, philosophers and high-income corporate swells surrounded me, although I learned later that some English majors changed their minds and became doctors. I was trying to figure all that out. In the process, I watched and listened as much to my classmates and other students as I did to any professor.

Millville was far from flawless. So was Holy Cross. And so was American society, which encompassed my world, whether or not I realized all the damaging waves those flaws swept over the land. Jackie Robinson, the courageous and great baseball player, and all those who followed him, represented most of the diversity that existed in Millville. Even that diversity was distant until the Boston Red Sox, New England's big league team, signed Elijah "Pumpsie" Green twelve long years after the Brooklyn Dodgers signed Robinson. Those Red Sox were the last major league team to add a Black player to its plantation. Millville was largely Irish-American, sprinkled with people of French-Canadian, Swedish, Polish and Lithuanian ancestry. My large Syrian-American family stood out in Millville, where every new resident was considered a "foreigner." Without realizing it until years later, I represented diversity in Millville. The same was true in college. One Black man, Tony Armstead graced my class at Holy Cross. Maybe four or five others were enrolled in the college in the late Fifties and early Sixties. The serious genesis of racial and social diversity was a decade away. Many would say that we, they, overcame. I say the struggle continues. A revolutionary shift in gender diversity reached Holy Cross, a historically all-male fortress, when women were admitted in the early 1970s. The usual exculpatory explanation for such previously backward behavior was, well, that was the way things were back then. True enough. But that's a white, male person's view. To outsiders it was a lame explanation for a few centuries of racism or worse. My self-contained diversity, in time, proved to be an asset as I roamed the world from Ireland to Afghanistan and in North and East Africa. I was able to fit in wherever I worked and be mistaken for many people I wasn't.

Hitching isn't all that's changed since 1958. College tuition was $700 in both my freshman and sophomore years. What a deal! Holy Cross was and remains a top-notch liberal arts college. Dr. Anthony Fauci, long the nation's Hippocrates on infectious diseases such as COVID-19, was a classmate. Tony Fauci lived on campus, but I've forgiven him for that. Epistemology was one of my favorite subjects. It was probably one of Fauci's too, judging from the clarity and wisdom with which he explained the truths and falsehoods of HIV and Covid-19, and the early ignorant presidential politics around it, to the American public.

I earned most of my tuition by working twelve weeks each summer at a mill that dyed wool and cotton on the banks of the Blackstone River in Woonsocket, Rhode Island. One of my uncles, my mother's oldest brother and a big boss, got me the job. On one very sleepy Saturday morning, after a very long Friday night, my uncle found me napping in a large box where wool was stored and very large river rats ruled. I was yelled at, but not fired. Uncles, like grandfathers, could also be good friends. By my senior year, tuition had risen to a whopping $1,000 a year, still not enough to overwhelm my summer earnings. My share of the gasoline for rides from Uxbridge to

Worcester and sometimes back to Uxbridge had been a princely $2 a week. The last time I peeked, tuition alone, absent room and board, had risen to $54,050 a year. My calls to the Saudis about the future of gas prices have gone unanswered.

In my first two years of college, I was enrolled in the Air Force Reserve Officers' Training Corps. That was my secret weapon, my only one. As a reward, I was issued a uniform. I wore that uniform three days a week for drills and classes about the Air Force. Often, I wore the uniform when I didn't have classes or drills. You had to be there to understand that an Air Force uniform was a ticket to more successful hitching. The uniform was also warm and welcome on winter days and nights when I found myself alone and wondering whether I'd reach home before it was time to head back to class.

Posing as a warrior defending the country wasn't a liability in 1958: it was a distinct advantage. For most Americans with even a clue, Vietnam was a sour soup known as French Indo-China. Another decade passed before Vietnam became a spoiled stew under Presidents Johnson and Nixon. Iran, Iraq and Afghanistan came later. Decades, maybe half a century, have passed since I've seen anyone, man or woman, wearing military garb standing on the verge with a thumb out.

After two years of counting and cursing drivers who ignored me, and tricking motorists into believing I was a vet, I got lucky. My grandfather gave me a car. My pale green 1950 Ford sedan with a broken driver's seat drove me from the curb to a classroom in the school of self-taught auto mechanics. To keep my car humming, I learned enough tricks to bail me out in Syria, decades later.

My Fifty Ford was no Ferrari, but it had an engine, four wheels, a gas pedal, brakes, clutch, shift and a steering wheel.

With the hood up, you could see more asphalt than car parts. Only the small engine, radiator, battery and critical master cylinder blocked the view. Not until I mastered its many quirks did I realize that my stripped down Ford was better than sticking my thumb out every day.

For starters, the flywheel was missing two teeth. When the missing teeth were aligned with the starter, the car wouldn't start.

"Shift into second gear," Rudy, my local mechanic, advised me, "go to the front of the car and rock it until the flywheel moves enough to engage its good teeth with the starter." That worked, if I were on level ground and wasn't wearing a cummerbund. To avoid that complication on big date nights, I parked on a hill where no other car could park in my face. Parking obstacles avoided, I would let the car roll down the hill with the clutch in and shift into second gear. When I let the clutch up quickly, the car would jerk and, presto, the engine would start. That was called popping the clutch, auto mechanics 101, back in 1958. I thought my date would never notice, although usually I thought wrong.

If the flywheel wasn't a crippling flaw, the master cylinder came close. It leaked, which could have been tragic. The master cylinder holds brake fluid. No brake fluid, no brakes. No brakes, a can't-miss crash. In the spring of 1962, six months before my Ford and I split, the master cylinder began to leak like a dripping faucet. That's when Rudy took me aside and whispered.

"Water," he said, "works just as well as brake fluid, and saves money," water being free back then. "But don't use water in winter," wise Rudy said. "And be sure to check the water regularly." Hell, I knew that, or what is college for? In September of 1962, just before I moved to test graduate school at Boston College, I junked my 1950 Ford before winter junked it for me. Boston was a breeze. So long leaky master cylinder and flawed flywheel. Hello mass transit.

OO

Dickie and Mr. Berkowitz trusted me, and I trusted them. We knew each other and our families. Even the strangers who stopped for me, a stranger hitching home from classes on Socrates, Plato and Aristotle trusted me, and I trusted them. That was a different time, a moment when there was more trust among people and within society. There were fewer cars and people then and more people without a car, so the need was more widely understood. Some drivers took pity on students with books slung over their shoulder and their thumbs out, begging. Trust, even a modicum of unspoken faith in humanity, is required to beg for a lift by the roadside. In the same way, trust in humanity is required for a driver to stop for a total stranger. We don't think about it in the same way, but trust is also needed to board a plane, hop on a bus or subway car, call Uber or Lyft or hail a taxi. We trust the system we think we know. Boarding a plane where passengers can haul chickens and stand in the aisle requires so much trust it's better not to think in such terms. There's no system to trust anyway, only humanity. The same is true about escaping across a wide, wild river on a homemade raft, bailing a leaky rowboat to find a war, or paying $1,000 to bounce senselessly past the graves of other journalists to apparent safety in another unsafe land. Without trust — much of which has been lost in America — life would be immobilized by fear. In unfamiliar lands, mutual needs replace trust as the currency of hitchhikers and motorists. Fighters seeking freedom in foreign lands happily ferry journalists to the next battle because they want the world to know their story. Driving a rental car, I've stopped for hitching soldiers in deserts because I wanted intelligence about their last battle, as well as the one just over the horizon. Those soldiers wanted to rest their tired feet but were also happy to tell their stories.

My two-years worth of hitching to and from college were relatively simple, safe and boring. But I never forgot that I needed a hitch more than drivers needed to stop for me. Those days weren't always easy, but trouble avoided me. Even the conversations were uninspiring. I learned to engage with strangers, to find out what interested them and to plumb for information and keep a conversation going. Without knowing it, I was getting an education on the road. In the late nineteen-fifties, hitching wasn't odd, and it was safe. The only weapon I ever carried in my youth was a compass, its needlepoint end serving as a small and probably useless tool for counterattacks. I carried this for my high school geometry class, but had to threaten its use only once, just before I fled from a suspicious driver on the back road between Milford and Millville. After geometry and I parted, I carried no weapon, small or large.

Pursuit of a career and raising a family became my life after college. Three years teaching high school after graduate school were followed by the lure and magnetism of becoming an ink-stained wretch, a newspaperman, now grandly and universally called a journalist, although newspapers are running out of ink. But hitching wasn't required, not immediately, anyway. All I did was grind down shoe leather reporting on national political conventions, chasing corrupt politicians and corporate cheats, and leading the editorial page of what one future governor and presidential candidate called the most liberal newspaper in the country. The politician thought he was insulting me. His intended insult, to me, was pure praise.

As an American newspaper correspondent, hitching in foreign lands was more than a tad riskier than hitching to college. But the balance of need worked in my favor. Often, I desperately needed a lift, and my benefactors saw me as someone who would tell their stories. Even hitching into and from battle zones, I was weapon free. Hitching in dangerous regions where I had no choice was also an effective way to learn more about new people and places. It was an open door to learn more, and learn more accurately, about strangers than I could garner from talking to tribal leaders, diplomats or heads of state.

On the road in remote regions, I bummed rides, but was never a bum because I had lots of cash. Sometimes I simply had no choice but to bum rides. I always had more than enough cash to get myself into and out of trouble because Cox Newspapers, my employer, supplied the money. Only once in ten years was I robbed. That was in the airport in Tashkent, Uzbekistan. My plane to Moscow was beyond late, and the waiting area was overflowing with angry travelers. In the crush, a security guard lifted my wallet and took $400. I knew a security guard was the thief because I told one guard my wallet was missing. The thief could keep the money, I told the guard, if my wallet and everything else in it was returned. Within minutes, my wallet, minus only the cash, was leaning against a pillar five yards distant.

Hitching in unfamiliar territory is a balancing act, like weighing risk, need and trust on a delicate scale. Urgency or survival often is the deciding factor about whether to ride with a stranger or hide in a cave. If the risk is too great, better to be patient until a better choice comes around. If survival is on the line, no risk is too great.

OO

"*Yallah*," I said to the man behind the wheel of a wired together 1948 DeSoto. "Let's go," I repeated, to make sure he understood. Continuing in Arabic and English, I asked, "Can you take me to Nahr al Furat, the Euphrates River?"

"*Aiwa*," yes, the man replied.

To each other, we were strangers. I was on a street in the heart of Aleppo, Syria. The DeSoto, painted a stale desert tan, was more than forty years old. I was fifty. The man could be trusted; I could sense that. He seemed too poor not to be trusted. We would be on the road all day heading for one of the world's greatest rivers. With its nearby cousin, the Tigris, the Euphrates gave birth to Western Civilization and they remain an essential source of fresh water in the Middle East. Combined, both rivers drain more than 600,000 square miles. The mighty Blackstone River drains slightly fewer, not even 600 square miles. Turkey at the time had dammed the Euphrates to provide hydroelectric power north across the border. Until the lake behind the dam was filled, the Euphrates would be dry; all I wanted was to walk across the dry riverbed, a coup in my history-oriented mind.

In the last decade of the twentieth century, my college education, hitchhiking skills, and lessons from Rudy, my auto mechanic, meshed beautifully. My problem, although not the driver of the DeSoto's, was that his old car stalled each time it stopped. As I started to explain that the driver should try raising the hood and whack the starter each time the car quit, the driver reached under his seat, grabbed a large rubber mallet, sprang from the car to raise the hood and pounded the starter before being deafened by the horns of surrounding drivers. Bingo. He knew the drill, and I realized the world is full of Rudys, as it is of Henry Aarons, Tom Bradys and Albert Einsteins.

Soon, my DeSoto and I were off on an all-day drive to the Euphrates, eastward to Lake Assad and back to Aleppo, a workout for both driver and mallet, and my Arabic. Near a cement watchtower that guarded against invaders, old and new, I took a short stride over a trickle and stepped across the Euphrates. Not a drop of water touched me. At the river that was then a river in name only, I met a shotgun-armed dentist from Aleppo and his bird dog. The black and white hound dashed where the ducks and other waterfowl should have been. But the dentist never fired a shot, and there were no dead ducks for the dog to retrieve. No invaders either. The Great Syrian War, the Islamic State of Iraq and Syria, and a whole lot of bombing and dying lay two decades ahead.

Barney McNeil

Barney's Barn

Holy Cross College

1948 DeSoto

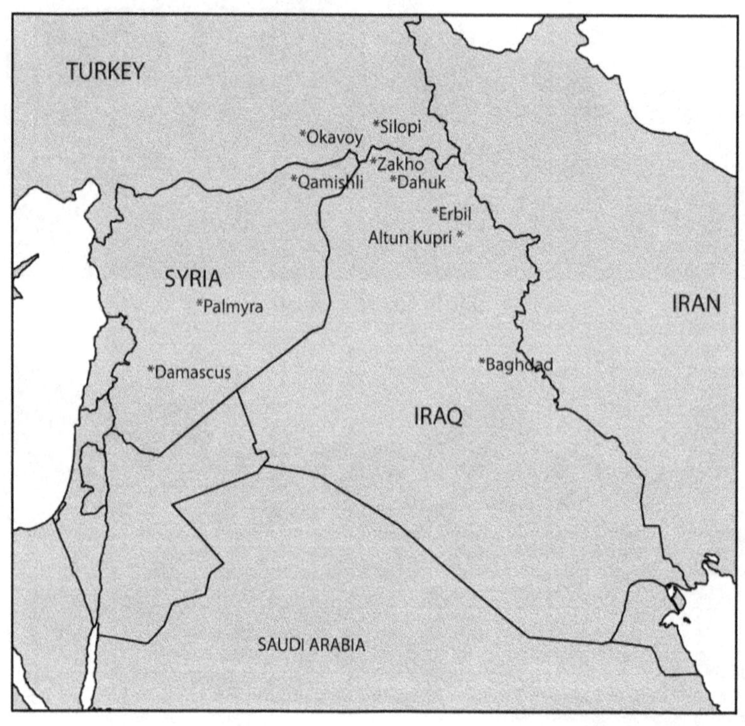
TURKEY
*Silopi
*Okavoy
*Zakho
*Qamishli
*Dahuk
*Erbil
Altun Kupri *
SYRIA
*Palmyra
IRAN
*Damascus
*Baghdad
IRAQ
SAUDI ARABIA

2 | FROM SYRIA TO IRAQ TO TURKEY

Martin, cameras dangling from straps around his neck, stared at me. I returned his wordless, quizzical gaze. Missiles, rockets or similar projectiles from Saddam Hussein's helicopters were aiming for humans and blasting dirt and boulders in a tightening circle around us. In time, maybe nanoseconds, a faceless stranger would have marked us as his bull's eye. It was pointless to hang around and watch the Iraqi Kurds get slaughtered. Quickly, Martin and I spoke and moved as one. We did an about face and headed toward a road a mile above the fray. In the long run, we would aim north for safety in Turkey, a tortuous journey as we found out. But it was a better bet than hitching almost two hundred miles straight south to Baghdad and into one of Saddam Hussein's prisons, or worse. Scrambling from the battlefield at Altun Kupri in northern Iraq, Martin and I headed to a ribbon of road where there was no blinking yellow light, and I wouldn't be waiting for a lift to college. The occasion was more existential.

"What now?" Martin and I asked each other when we reached the asphalt.

"We hitch, what else?" I answered. We weren't alone in our flight. With three others, locals all, we squeezed into a small car, a free ride and another hitch for me. The driver was going our way, bound for the city of Erbil, a safe haven an hour's drive north and a day, maybe two, ahead of the helicopters. Joining us was a young woman wearing a dress, not a battle dress, and high heels. She didn't carry a weapon either. What had a woman so attired been doing on a battlefield? First answer is that battlefields shield many secrets, some dead, others still pumping. Earlier, in the midst of the battle, I had spoken with an armed and seasoned twenty-five-year-old Kurdish woman, who said she was fighting to defend her brothers, in the broadest sense. Further, the Kurds are secular Sunni Muslims, not religious police like the Saudis or Iranian mullahs, and trained Kurdish women actually shoot to kill. A few months later, I watched Kurdish women from Turkey training for combat at a boot camp in Lebanon. Maybe that was the answer.

Martin Nangle and I met by chance at a hotel in Damascus, Syria's capital. A photographer from Belfast, Northern Ireland, he was working for the Associated Press. I was the Middle East correspondent for the Atlanta-based Cox Newspapers group. We shared the same goal: reach Iraq immediately after the end of the first Gulf War. That was when America's president, George Herbert Walker Bush, had urged Kurds in northern Iraq and Shiite Arabs in southern Iraq to rise up against Saddam Hussein. By the time Martin and I drifted from Syria to the battlefield in Iraq, we had learned enough to sense that the Kurds were doomed. Kurdish leaders, with their unyielding, extreme bravado, told us so, and their lack of heavy weapons confirmed our beliefs.

Planes, hired cars, even taxis in exhaust-choked Cairo — plus old-fashioned shoe leather — took me around the horn of three Middle East capitals before the first Gulf war began. A few months later, just after the war ended, old-fashioned hitching rescued Martin Nangle and me from an Iraqi battlefield. Iraq triggered this particular oil war when Saddam Hussein invaded neighboring Kuwait. Both countries were loaded with that dirty three-letter word — oil. In order to boot Iraq from Kuwait and punish Saddam Hussein for his insolence, the Arab dictatorships had to go along with — or at least not resist — Western war plans led by the United States and Father Bush. I was assigned to assess the popular mood and war preparations in Jordan, Egypt and the United Arab Emirates. Hiring a car, which is like hitching only it lightens the money belt, whisked me east from Jerusalem to the Jordan River. After my passport passed muster, another hired car, called a taxi, took me to Amman, Jordan's capital. After two weeks of reporting from Amman, I found Cairo by air. An American ally, Egypt would remain quiet, although the mood on the street differed radically from the mood in the tower of dictator Hosni Mubarak. Another plane took me to Dubai and Abu Dhabi in the United Arab Emirates. The Emirates also possessed barrels of that greasy three-letter word, and nothing and no one that would interfere with this war. Not wanting to miss the opening salvos, I returned in a circuitous route to Tel Aviv. My arrival matched that of the Iraqi Scud missiles.

When the first air raid sirens screamed over Israel, I was interviewing a foreign intelligence officer/diplomat at dinner in Jerusalem. The sirens scattered people and china, and I never saw the diplomat again, which probably pleased him but not his dinner companion. A few days later, I drove in my rental car with John Hockenberry, then with National Public Radio, to a burning textile factory near Ben Gurion airport. John and I reached the factory several minutes before anyone else. The night watchman greeted us outside the blazing building he was supposed to defend. But he was helpless against the Scuds. Firefighters, ready to fight poison gas, were enveloped in white tent-like garments and looked like moonwalkers or exorcists as they plodded to the scene well after John and I and the Scuds.

The war went as expected. Saddam's forces were routed. Saddam was allowed to stay in power to avoid the tribal and sectarian chaos that erupted a dozen years later when Bush Junior invaded Iraq to erase the weapons of mass destruction that didn't exist and plunge the United States into a desert of quicksand.

Soon after the first Gulf war ended, with Saddam Hussein still on his throne, Father Bush punched my ticket to Iraq. Off I went from Tel Aviv to northern Iraq. There's no four-lane highway that leads from one to the other, not even a jet stream or a dusty trail. My route was supposed to be by air from Tel Aviv north to Cyprus where I expected to receive documents that would help me hook up with Kurds in Turkey or Syria. Kurdish guides were to then shuttle me overland into northern Iraq's Kurdistan.

As with so many war plans, mine fell apart quickly, neatly. An agency in Cyprus that helped arrange visas and make connections in other countries struck out. Syria, on my own, became my best alternative. After my Cypriot connection arranged a Syrian visa, I was off to the wilderness of Damascus. Damascus isn't Iraq, but many Kurds live in northeast Syria near the border with Iraq. From Damascus I planned to find my way to Qamishli, a Kurdish city in northeastern Syria, close to the Tigris River that marks the border with Iraq. In Qamishli, I would have to meet Kurds who would take me to Iraq. The drive from Damascus to Qamishli is not a ride across town. And I wasn't going to meet old friends. It's a ten-hour hitch through the Great Syrian Desert and skirting the ancient Roman ruins of Palmyra.

Instant allies when we shook hands in Damascus, Martin and

I became friends in our search for the same fast trail to Iraq. If we arrived too late, we would miss the Kurdish uprising. If we missed the uprising, we would miss the rout and the story. As we later learned, even if we arrived in time for the uprising, the story would be stuck in the weeds with us on the banks of the Khabur River until we escaped on a raft, a last ditch hitch, from Iraq to Turkey, and reached phones.

Flying from Damascus was the fastest and least costly way to reach Qamishli. We arranged a flight, which in a flash was cancelled. Our only choice was to hire a car, which would cost seven times more than a flight. This was our Hobson's choice, which was no choice at all. After a few days lost to making those arrangements, we left Damascus on our daylong drive to Qamishli. Our driver was a hired gun, a member of the Syrian secret police, although he didn't wear a badge or flash a weapon. Throughout the Arab Middle East, the secret police are known as the *mukhabarat*. Our driver's official role was obvious because he was stationed at my French-owned hotel in Damascus. Further, he drove a late model Volvo, a signature of the secret police, which was in much better condition than the 1948 DeSoto that I plucked from an Aleppo street. No self-respecting taxi driver in Damascus drove a late model Volvo. Our driver's official status didn't trouble me because Martin and I were who we said we were. We had nothing to hide, and we needed a car that could reach Qamishli. If nothing else, we would feel secure in the Volvo. If our watchdog expected us to pull guns and demand that he veer off so we could sabotage the oil fields, he would have been disappointed. Further, the Syrian regime at the time, headed by Hafez Al-Assad, was no friend of Iraq's Saddam Hussein. Both Assad and Hussein were dictators. Syria would not and did not stand in the way of anyone who wished to watch trouble pummel its next-door dictator.

My Arabic tongue, which stuck to familiar talk about the delicious Arabic food I ate growing up, was creative until we reached the Great Syrian Desert. By then, my kitchen Arabic became repetitive and boring, even to me. Martin left the food talk to me.

The desert is beautiful, especially at night, in total darkness without ambient light and under a sky of limitless stars that seemed to stretch from pole to pole. We counted sand pebbles, dunes and rocks until we reached the town of Tadmor on the eastern edge of Palmyra's ruins, more than three hours from Damascus and seven more turns of the hour hand from Qamishli. On a bend in the asphalt, we stopped to digest desert dust along with French fries, chicken kabobs and salad at a small roadside storefront before driving on. As we ate, I thought of Queen Zenobia, whose empire the Romans had trashed so they could build their ruins.

Without incident and long after burping our way past Palmyra and the kabobs, Martin and I were lost in Qamishli, heavily populated with Kurds. The next day we would search for Kurdish guides and a hitch into Iraq. Choosing sleep over dinner, we took a room for the night in a rickety building that posed as a hotel. A three-alarm blaze in the hall outside our room snapped us to attention hours before the muezzin woke the faithful for dawn prayers. Local pharmacists cooking drugs had accidentally ignited a roaring fire that they extinguished faster than Martin and I thought possible when we stepped into the hall ready to flee before we roasted. With nowhere else to turn, we decided to return to snoring, each with one eye open and both ears at the ready. On schedule, the prayer-chanting muezzin woke us at dawn. Soon after the sun rose, we knocked on the door of the local police, figuring they might show the foreign press the way to Syria's unfriendly Iraq. We were right. Each of us had something the other wanted. Flush with a variety of phones that connected Syria to the outside world, the local gendarme opened those phones to Martin and me. The captain, who proudly said he had a relative, a doctor, living in Providence, Rhode Island, also embraced Martin's Irish connection. Middle Easterners who aren't Israelis generally love Irlanda because they see brother combatants—Irish Republicans battling the British occupiers as the Palestinians resist Israeli occupation. Martin called his wife in Northern Ireland, and I called my wife back in Massachusetts, and my office in Washington. Those were wake-up calls about where we were and where we were headed, which was about to become more than a travel story.

Soon after daybreak we were on the dusty road to the nearby village of Al-Malikiyah, a short toss to the Tigris River. On the opposite bank lay Iraq. On both sides of the Tigris, Martin and I were in the hands of the Kurds. We wanted to tell the story of their fight against Saddam Hussein, and they wanted to use us to tell the world of their eternal campaign for an independent state. Until we fled with our Kurdish hosts toward Turkey almost two weeks later, Martin and I and fourteen other journalists relied on the Kurds for our safety and sustenance. Despite the dangers and the severity of their losses, the Kurds never failed us.

Hitching again, Martin and I bounced high in a military personnel truck heading to the Tigris. Along the way, four large bottles of water flew from my lap and burst at our feet. A dozen oranges and large bags of pistachios and almonds survived to nourish us for days. With us were two Kurds from Germany and a German woman, along with the Kurdish truck driver. The trio from Germany said they worked in radio. Hello, I thought, and I'm reporting for the *Martian Daily Chronicle.* If I had to say precisely who arranged our transportation to the Tigris and beyond, I couldn't. If I had to guess, I would finger the Syrian security services working with local Kurds. This was the deal: we would cross the Tigris from where Iraqi Kurds would take us to a high spot on the dirt road. There, we would stay off the roadsides to avoid mines, and wait for Iraqi Kurds to shepherd us to the city of Zakho in northern Iraq. First, we had to hitch across the Tigris. This was my first riverboat hitch, but not my last, not even my most risky, although it was hardly a first-class crossing. A small rowboat with a half horsepower engine met us on the Syrian side of the Tigris. The boat leaked, something like a large colander used to drain water from pounds of cooked spaghetti. We didn't relish the image, especially because water from the Tigris was seeping into our colander. We reached Iraq without sinking. Then we walked, waited and sang Kurdish fight songs with our new hosts until more Kurds arrived to drive us to the Kurdish city of Zakho. We reached Zakho without stepping on or driving over a land mine. There, we watched the Kurds prepare for a war they could not and would not win. They won small psychological battles, but nothing more. Brave fighters, used to fighting, usually losing and often being betrayed by allies and themselves, the Kurds talked only of winning as they waved rifles and other small arms, their weapons of failure.

Little time passed before Martin and I met fourteen other journalists on the same mission. We were a small force from six countries with no battlefield weapons. Our joint but separate mission was to learn whether the Kurds were as doomed as we were coming to believe. Telling the world what happened to the Kurds would be even more difficult than finding the story because we lacked any means of communication. For several days, we gathered information from Kurdish fighters and their leaders in Zakho and the nearby Kurdish city of Dahuk. We heard of their plans and hopes, and counted their small weapons and larger guns that hadn't worked since the last war.

To get the story and tell it, the Kurds needed us and we needed them. Hitching rides around town was easy. No fees attached. Soon it became apparent that the story, the battle, would be farther south near the city of Erbil. That was a hitch of a different distance. Weighed down by audio and video equipment, for theirs is an audio/visual show-and-tell medium, a crew of four CNN journalists required a van for transportation. The rest of our squad, in another form of hitching, kicked in shares of the transportation costs. One late afternoon we rumbled south through the green hills of northern Iraq and into the long night from Dahuk southeast to Erbil. When the driver lost his way and headed into the teeth of a serious Iraqi force near Mosul, CNN's night vision camera saved us from becoming statistics. A U-turn was in order, not long before our van quit. A broken fan belt, the driver said. But don't worry, he announced, he'd go and fetch one. Our driver vanished, leaving his muddled passengers with no idea where they were or where he was headed. In less than an hour, our driver returned with a new fan belt or an adequate poseur. Off we drove until we needed another fan belt. The drill was the same. Our driver announced the fan belt problem, said he was off to find another, and left. Somehow, he returned, victorious, again. On and on we drove in the darkness. Normally a six-hour trip, our wilderness trek took sixteen. We left Dahuk before dinner on one day and reached Erbil just in time for eggs, olives, tea and bread the day after. The big battle in Altun Kupri was coming closer to us, and we were gaining on it, thanks to a successful all-night, multi-fan-belt hitch.

After the Kurds lost Altun Kupri along with many lives, the CNN crew stumbled into Erbil the next morning. Martin and I greeted them with questions; their answers were fresh but as we expected. They had more audio-video grist than Martin and I, but were unhappy because days would pass before their news, and ours, would serve any purpose. Until our ragged squad could flee Iraq, we were all stuck with a story we could only tell to each other. The Iraqi army had shut down the Tigris crossing to Syria. That left thousands of Kurds fleeing east to Iran or north to Turkey. We had zero desire to shake hands with the supreme leader in Iran. No one among us voted to hike two hundred miles south toward Baghdad and into Saddam Hussein's clutches. Speechless, we headed the hundred or so miles toward Turkey, the high road we later called it, without knowing of the jagged peaks and mechanical disasters that lay ahead — a series of vehicles that broke down as another ached for rest on a road swallowed in mud atop steep cliffs a step from a raging river. For a couple of days our pack broke up, stumbled and bumbled our way from Erbil. Separately, we found cars, drivers and enough gasoline to speed us past Kurdish checkpoints toward the Turkish border only to have our car quit. After the driver of one of our cars stopped to kiss his wife goodbye, we hit the right road north in the right cars. The Kurds helped us as much as possible, but they had larger problems: they had to save themselves.

When all sixteen of us, more by accident than strategic planning, reached a Kurdish mountaintop citadel, the Kurds deemed our two Toyota Land Cruisers too small to cross the mountains, rivers, and muddied and blocked gravel pits that lay ahead. In a short time, in most improbable circumstances, we found a driver with a ten-wheel truck who drove us to Zakho, a harrowing sixteen-hour stop-and-stumble drive north. Something about a broken fan belt apparatus, the driver said, forced him to quit in Zakho. He refused to take us to the Khabur River, which marks the Turkish-Iraqi border. We were still a broken-down minivan, a military transport and a long march from the Khabur, where a few Kurdish peshmerga fighters — Kurdish meaning those who face death — would do their best to shelter themselves and us before the peshmergas fled to avoid Saddam's deliverance. We were heading to Turkey, come hell or the high waters of the Khabur.

Martin Nangle was one of four in our group who volunteered to swim across the Khabur River into the unwelcoming arms of Turkish soldiers. No one held a gun to the heads of our swimmers. The bullets came later. At best a wader and never a swimmer, I volunteered to say nothing more except that I wouldn't launch my swimming career by attempting a paddle to Turkey. Send help when you reach the other side, I said to the volunteers, meaning Turkey, not heaven. Our first two swimmers—Jim Hill, a CNN reporter, and the late Xavier Gauthier, then with the Paris daily *Le Figaro*—reached Turkey because the Turks fired in a wide circle around them. Martin and his swimming partner, Rich Brooks, also with CNN, were forced to swim back to Saddam's land because the bullets circled closer to their skins, which they didn't want to lose. Xavier Gauthier was critical to the rescue of the remaining fourteen of our cohort who stayed stuck in the Iraqi mud. Gauthier knew the local governor of the Turkish province where he had washed ashore.

A day later, two Turks wearing shorts, T-shirts and one sporting a blue blazer — sans cummerbund — towed a makeshift raft across the Khabur for the rest of us. Hitching on that raft — which was stitched together by truck-sized inner tubes, orange crate staves and brown plastic television antenna wires of yore — was riskier than crossing the Tigris in a leaky rowboat. But it was a risk that had to be taken. After ferrying fourteen desperate journalists in two separate trips, our two Turkish rescuers sailed us into the arms of Turkish authorities at the lip of Ova Koy, a nearby village. Wet, cold and hungry, Martin and I and our colleagues caught up with Xavier Gauthier and Jim Hill, who by this time had dried out. Our hitching, aided by Turkish authorities who wanted us gone, continued. Half our tribe was taken to the larger town of Silopi in an armored personnel carrier; the other half rode in an open military truck. We used a heater in a large room to dry our clothes before the Turks took another step up humanity's ladder. They fed us as Welcome Wagon greeters would new neighbors. We toasted our Turkish rescuers and feasted on a mess of bread, cheese, hard-boiled eggs, olives, tahini, bottled water and tea. Along the way out of the town and country, we stayed in a hotel where we could file stories and were processed in court as illegal border-crossers. The government, in a sleight of hand, said it paid our fines for entering the country illegally. Our rescuers knew how we had entered Turkey, but they were puzzled about how we had entered Iraq because our passports showed no Iraqi stamps. We didn't tell the Turks that there had been no passport office in the Iraqi mud when Martin and I floated across the Tigris from Syria to meet the Kurds.

Our exit from Turkey to Syria was smoother and drier than crossing the Tigris River into Iraq or rafting across the Khabur from Iraq to Turkey.

Finding transportation from Qamishly — where Martin and I

had stashed personal items before we entered Iraq — to Damascus was another taste of transportation torture. Flight plans fell through after a six-hour delay. We abandoned an old, belching car that seemed like a bad bet to make the ten-hour drive to Damascus. We paid the driver a pittance in Syrian pounds for his trouble. Lucky once more, we flagged an unscheduled bus that wasn't belching. After stops for midday and evening prayers in the Great Syrian Desert, before and after which I wowed our guardian soldiers with stories about growing up on Arabic food in America, Damascus was ours at four the next morning. That wasn't exactly what I would call a clean escape. It was, however, slightly smoother than our entry into Iraq. But I learned far more about the Kurds in Syria and Iraq by hitching in its many forms than I would have had I flown calmly in and out of Saddam Hussein's killing fields.

Kurds in Erbil armed for the battle at Altun Kupri

Photographer Martin Nangle with Kurdish fighter.

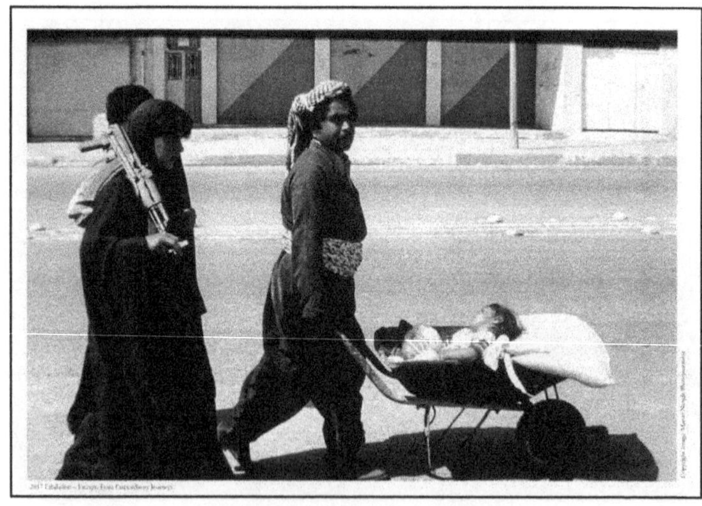

Erbil, Iraqi Kurdish Uprising

Peshmerga fighter in Iraqi Kurdistan

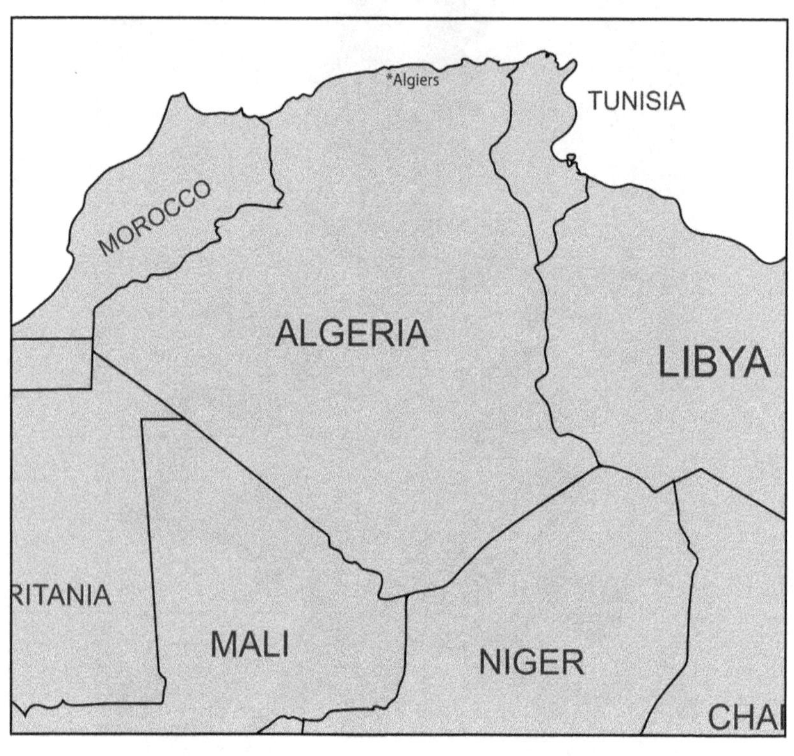
*Algiers
TUNISIA
MOROCCO
ALGERIA
LIBYA
RITANIA
MALI
NIGER
CHA

3 | HITCHING INTO THE CASBAH

Algeria was shedding blood in a diabolically uncivil civil war when the tip reached me in London. Along with other journalists, I would have the opportunity to take a peek at the forbidden country in the forbidding Sahara. Reaching Africa's largest country was difficult. Finding the truth, though messy, was easier. An impending election was supposed to quiet widespread criticism of the war and herald the advent of a long-delayed democracy. Oddly enough, suspended elections five years earlier had triggered the war. Coming my way was an invitation to witness the military junta's version of the truth, so I was eager to see how reality stacked up against the political message.

A Canadian friend with connections in Algiers tipped me off. "Get in line," my friend said, "and you'll get a visa." He couldn't say when. Getting in line meant applying for a visa and waiting, waiting. First, I tempered my eagerness in London, where I was based in 1997. For three weeks, daily, I called the Algerian embassy in Paris to check on my visa. Several times I met personally with Algerian diplomats hoping to speed the process. Sometimes I flew to Paris, where visas were being issued, just to let the Algerians know that I still had a pulse. Other times I took the Chunnel, the train under the English Channel, to France. Those were not my usual forms of hitchhiking. A version of the standard method came later.

While loitering in London, I interviewed human rights

advocates whose knowledge of the chaos in Algeria proved the best available. Most important were the names, addresses and telephone numbers of lawyers and other human rights advocates in Algeria. Without that information, etched carefully in two notebooks, I would have been lost in Algiers, forced to fathom the truth from information that only the government and the army provided.

Anticipating the go-ahead, I packed and bivouacked in Paris for a few days, a hardship like no other, so I'd be ready to fly immediately after an Algerian visa was stamped into my thick blue U.S. passport. Fortune, good or bad, would find me landing in Algiers among strangers, to be watched, guarded, by soldiers and the police. My secret ally turned out to be the intelligence that I picked up in London. That intelligence led me to meet a man I would come to call a friend. The moment, too, was perfect for polishing my hitchhiking skills. A few fellow journalists left Algiers on arrival because they had made no friendly connections. Because I was informed, luck rode in my shoulder bag.

The army garrisoned all visiting journalists in the same hotel, the El Aurassi, high on a hillside overlooking the whitewashed city, its port and the sparkling Mediterranean. Height and distance painted Algiers with a false patina of alabaster freshness. The cemeteries and the keening survivors of war were outside the capital city, hidden among palm trees and fruit groves in smaller towns and villages, some on the edges of the great Sahara or the towering Atlas Mountains.

When the army decided we should see where mass killings occurred, our trailing troop of inquisitors stepped into a convoy of three vans, one mini-bus and one car. Although we were journalists to whom uniforms were anathema, we appeared to be soldiers from just another brigade as real colonels drove us from one devastated village to another. The army's message was that Islamist fighters killed their betrayers in those villages. But that's not all we heard. Some villagers told us that uniformed soldiers did the killing, or did nothing to stop it. The military junta put the war and its unrelenting massacres all on the Islamic fundamentalists. For several days, we heard conflicting stories with the same theme: good guys don't exist in this war.

Inside the El Aurassi the police policed us, the visiting truth-tellers. Outside the city, the burden of vigilance fell to the army. One day the military relented, its soft spot supposedly exposed. With a few other journalists, I was allowed to enter the city center, called the casbah, a thick warren of thin alleys, streets and buildings that embraced each other more in self-defense than love. A half-dozen security officers, dark glasses stuck to their faces, stayed in sight as I walked on rooftops to watch women and their daughters prepare food. The watchdogs followed as I strolled the streets and talked with shopkeepers and jobless young men who leaned on buildings and in doorways. "What about the elections?" I asked. "Will you vote?" Without exception the answers were that no one trusted the integrity of the upcoming elections, and no one trusted the military junta – the High Command – to conduct a free and fair election.

"The government always wins, so why should we vote?" a man told me.

No one talked too long or said too much because they could see the plainclothes officers tailing me and eyeing them. That was the idea. Give foreign correspondents a whiff of Algeria's freedom by allowing them to talk with regular folks, but do so under close guard. What would seem like real freedom to interview local people wasn't freedom at all, and the people knew it.

Hotel walls were supposed to contain the foreign press and prevent us from seeing what we weren't supposed to see. Guided tours to sites of massacres — twenty-four members of an extended family were murdered in one village — were to act as another blanket to conceal the truth. But walls don't always do their designated jobs. Within the El Aurassi's whitewashed walls, my new friend and I hatched a plan that would allow me to meet with humanitarian lawyers, activists, and victims of those who were fighting the military government, and mostly losing. Armed with a decades-old experience grounded in hitchhiking, I was ready to break the rules. From the start, I trusted my new friend, partly because the people I interviewed in London said I could and partly because intuition said I should. I became adept at judging people while hitching during my first two years of college, and I polished that skill for years on three other continents. Risks and rewards were there to be taken and seized when needed and when the odds, I judged, seemed to be in my favor. Early on I trusted my new friend because he had more to lose than I did if things went awry. If caught, my destination probably wouldn't be the Algerian gulag. Rather, I'd be shoved onto a plane bound for Paris. Those were guesses, risks, that I was willing to take to round out the story. My friend's destination, if he were caught, wouldn't have been Paris.

Early one afternoon, when an army tour wasn't planned, I casually drifted from the pack to a far corner of the hotel wall. On the street outside, my friend, experienced in the art and science of journalism and who reported for news outlets outside of Algeria, was waiting. We were to meet at an appointed time, and speed off to interview opposition leaders whom I was not supposed to know existed. The hotel wall wasn't the Great Wall of China or a wall surrounding a medieval city. Nor was climbing the wall like walking straight out the hotel door or waiting for Dickie McCrohan or Mr. Berkowitz to pick me up at Millville's blinking amber light. I scaled the lowest end of the wall as planned, met my friend on the street outside, and we were off. Without the guidance of my new friend, the rest of Algeria's grim story would have remained hidden from me.

His office was tiny and cluttered, as it had to be. Mohammed reminded me of an American criminal defense lawyer whose clients were all on Death Row, or on their way. I met Mohammed alone; my friend parked out of sight while our security attachés were left behind watching other journalists at the El Aurassi. In short order, Mohammed introduced a client, a former high school principal who described in awful and painful detail how his testicles had been cut off in a prison he called "the door of the desert." The wounded man told his story of torture and lightless cells. He was, the man said, locked away and brutalized for almost five years, beginning in 1992. Mohammed picked up the larger story. In 1995 all human and legal rights protections were wiped out when the military junta eliminated special courts designed to hear only terrorism and security cases. No courts, no defendants. As a result, Mohammed said, prisoners simply disappeared. Mohammed counted four lawyers among the 12,000 Algerians who had disappeared in the nineties. Though difficult to nail down, Mohammed put the death toll at 400,000 to 500,000, including sixty-five journalists.

Shortly before she received the European Parliament's Sakharov Prize for Freedom of Thought, I walked in unannounced on Salima Ghozali. Finding her wasn't easy, but that's what new friends are for. Ghozali was on the run from authorities. She moved constantly from house to house and sent her two daughters to live with her sister far from Algiers. Her newspaper, *La Nation*, was shut down because she owed the government printing office $100,000. Hers was the country's only independent newspaper at the time, and the government was her only printer. The government had cornered and silenced Ghozali, who was also a leader of Algeria's women's rights movement.

Later, with the Sakharov Prize as a shield, Ghozali had a bit more glossy protection from the state, the army and unofficial critics. But praise from outsiders offers little shelter from internal intimidation. A target of unrelenting threats never feels free enough to live without fear. Ghozali closed our long conversation with these words: "The generals are afraid of people like me, a little person. So that is some consolation."

Salima Ghozali wasn't without sister allies: Louiza Hanoun was one of them. With my new friend and guide leading the way, I met Hanoun, leader of the Algerian Workers' Party, in her office. At the time, Hanoun was the only woman leading a political party in the Arab world. Without help, advice and my extended hitchhiking skills, I never would have found Hanoun, who was also fighting for the freedom of women and for her country. Many women, an uncertain number as high as 500, had been killed during the war, simply because they were women. An untold number of women were in prison simply because they were married to Islamists, real or suspected. She learned about imprisoned women, Hanoun said, only after their families sought help. Islamists killed some women because they *refused* to wear a veil. Security forces killed other women because they *did* wear a veil.

Algeria's civil war grew clearer after that day of interviews ended. On another level, clarity was possible because my new friend and I took calculated risks. We judged each other correctly. Satisfied, my friend and I bought street food before we headed back to the El Aurassi. I stepped from the car several blocks from the hotel. Then I ambled casually into the lobby as if I belonged there and had never left. Strolling through the lobby I thought of my walk through the corridors of British intelligence in London. Instead of pinning an ID badge on my lapel, as required, I stuffed it my pocket. No one questioned me. I was suitably dressed, so everyone who passed seemed to view me as being so high up the food chain that I didn't need a badge.

El Aurassi Hotel
Photo: Ludovic Courtès – Creative Commons, 2008

Salima Ghozali, 1997 European Parliament

The author in Algeria

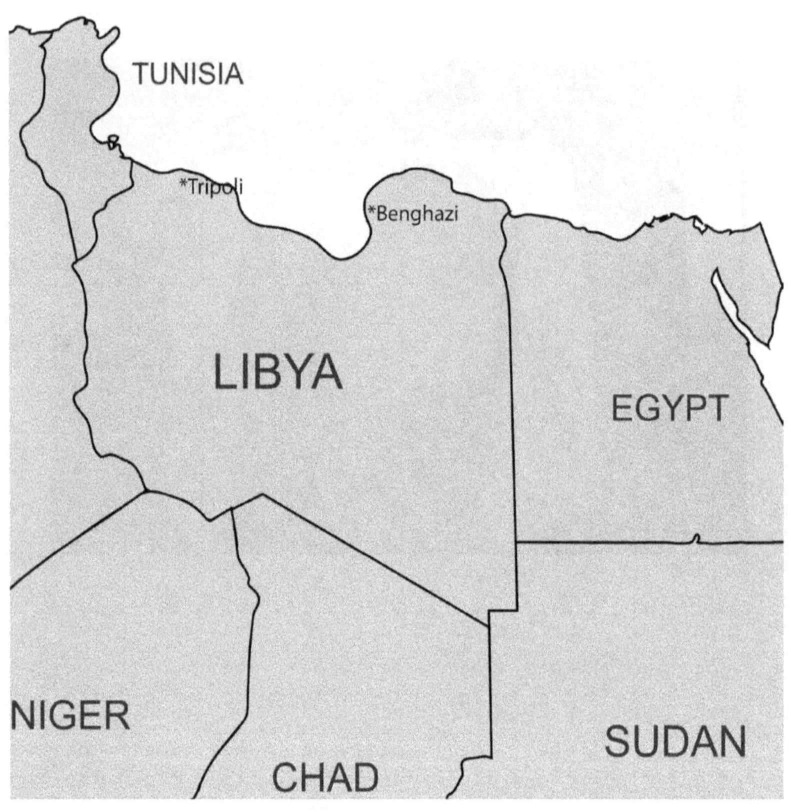
TUNISIA
*Tripoli
*Benghazi
LIBYA
EGYPT
NIGER
CHAD
SUDAN

4 | ESCAPING FROM ROOM 119

"Your room is number 119. You can go there," said the mouth just below the dark glasses. Tall and broad-shouldered, I had no intention of trifling with the man, no matter his size or social skills. This was his country, a dictatorship. I was a visitor, a snoopy journalist. We were cloistered on a ship, and the journalists on board seemed intent on avoiding open rebellion unless the food was fifth-rate. Though ever-present and hovering, security wasn't hostile. Tripoli, Libya's capital on the southern shore of the sultry Mediterranean, was to be my home port to witness a dictator's pat on his own back. With other visiting journalists too numerous to count, I was in town to observe and write about the twentieth anniversary of Muammar Qaddafi's rise to power. Twenty years earlier, in 1969, Qaddafi led a coup that overthrew King Idris I, now remembered by few outside his immediate family. Should the rest of the world forget his revolutionary success, Qaddafi was hosting a three-day personal parade that was part carnival and wholly a reminder of who was in charge.

Qaddafi and his extenuating rebels were on good behavior, which the journalists were invited to witness. Over the years, Qaddafi's name has been spelled or misspelled more often than Yasser Arafat's and the Grand Ayatollah Sayyid Ruhollah Mousavi Khomeini's combined. But getting the spelling straight was nothing compared to understanding the revolutionary slogans that plastered the ship's interior and decorated Green

Square, Tripoli's heart where festivities honoring "The Leader" were held.

"Democracy means popular rule. Not popular expression. The most tyrannical dictatorships the world has known existed under the shadow of parliaments." Twelve other muscular revolutionary expressions festooned the walls of the ship's main lobby. The city itself was busy with Qaddafi's face, the number 20 shining in bright lights on his dictatorship, although his intent was to show a more pragmatic face to the West without alienating his allies, such as Syria and the Palestine Liberation Organization.

In the autumn of 1989, Qaddafi was still walking with a metaphorical limp and a wounded heart due to the American bombing in 1986 of Tripoli and Benghazi, Libya's second city. Ronald Reagan had ordered the attacks because of Qaddafi's alleged support of terrorist strikes against American interests and a variety of other missteps, such as Qaddafi being Qaddafi. Qaddafi's fifteen-month-old adopted daughter was killed in the attack on his residence, and his two young sons were injured by seeing-eye missiles. But the autumn of 1989 was not the end of Qaddafi's life or of his time on the throne. Libya's fatal revolution against "The Leader's" long rule remained more than two decades away, in a new century. Cornered in his home district of Sirte in the fall of 2011, Qaddafi was killed by his own people, a NATO bomb, or a combination of both.

My time to enter Room 119 had come. When it did, I wasn't alone. To my surprise, another journalist had also booked a bunk in Room 119. A chance to learn a little, I thought, because I had been in the region only six months. My roommate was a journalist with Egypt's main newspaper, *Al-Ahram* (The Pyramids). That's what he told me, and I believed him. Whatever else he was didn't matter to me. *Al-Ahram* remained one of the most independent, though less so than it had been, and influential newspapers in the Arab world, Cairo being the capital of the most populous Arab country.

Pleasantries aside, my roommate and I talked about the strength of Qaddafi's control over Libya, and of Egyptian-Libyan relations. After ten years of hostilities, relations between Libya and Egypt were on the upswing. Egypt, Libya's immediate neighbor to the east, sent its deputy prime minister to Qaddafi's party, a nod but not a deep bow to "The Leader." A dictatorship itself, Egypt wasn't warm to a revolutionary dictator next door, a man who could be troublesome. In Qaddafi's eyes, Egypt's peace with Israel made it difficult for an Arab nationalist like him to embrace the Pharaohs' successors. As the Egyptian newsman, my roommate, viewed "The Leader," Qaddafi the ideologue was attempting to show himself as a pragmatist, easing his support for organizations accused of being terrorists first and freedom fighters second, and slowly opening Libya's economy to the West. Diplomats and Libyan academics later told me a similar story. Libyan shop owners and customers told me of their desires to sell to and purchase more products from the West.

On the ship and on the streets, security was tight but not oppressive. Traffic in the capital was light, by design. Cars that buzzed through the city center were driven by Qaddafi's security. Real taxis didn't exist; they were occupied by the *mukhabarat,* the secret police.

Bumming a ride in Tripoli was nothing like hailing a taxi in Moscow when the Soviet Union was collapsing. Only a pack of American cigarettes held high brought a taxi to a screeching halt near Moscow's Red Square. Even a handful of American dollars didn't work, especially at night, because it was difficult to distinguish useless rubles from American cash. But American cigarette brands glowed in the dark.

If you stood on a street in Tripoli, a security-driven car posing as a taxi would stop whether or not you hailed the driver. Courtesy and control worked well together.

Fortunately, my roommate didn't stay the night. He had an eye infection that needed treatment, or so he said. We wished each other well when my roommate left before dinner. He talked a lot, but never asked one question.

The twentieth anniversary of his rise to power created perfect conditions for Qaddafi and company. He could let in as many journalists as wished to enter the closed country. By putting them on a ship where they could be watched most of the time, Qaddafi could watch them most of the time. He could set up a press center so his guests could file stories with ease, arrange time-consuming tours that never happened or, when they did, allowed journalists to see only what the regime wanted them to see, which was usually nothing. From a journalist's perspective, those arrangements were the best on the table. The alternative was to remain on the ship and wonder about Qaddafi's super project in the vast desert, the Great Man-Made River Project.

When Libyan security wanted to move the ship's passengers, it did so without warning. Returning from the press center after filing a story, I found that the ship itself had gone AWOL. After scrambling to locate the ghost ship, or at least to recover my toothbrush and comb, order was restored when I found all of my luggage and papers on the curb next to a large motel. Other journalists were just as fortunate.

In the mix of this planned convenience and confusion, Qaddafi's good humor forces weren't well organized for their moment in the sun. Several European diplomats spoke of having planned meetings with Libyan officials cancelled at the last moment. Even meetings with Qaddafi's allies in the region were either cancelled or held with little consequence. No questions were answered; no explanations were given. An important trip was scheduled for journalists early one morning. A convoy of buses was to pick up journalists well before dawn that day. The buses and journalists showed up, but the trip was cancelled without explanation. No one knew where we were supposed to go or what we were to see. But journalists were ready because the chance to see something you don't have an opportunity to see in a dictatorship doesn't happen every morning.

My opportunity to bolt from the herd came when a half-the-night and all-day bus trip was scheduled to see Qaddafi's Great Man-Made River Project deep in the Sahara. This was the secret and vast network of aqueducts, pipelines and reservoirs that everyone wanted to spy. Started in 1983 and still going though crippled by civil war, the project brings fresh but centuries old water from deep down in the desert to Libya's coastal cities where most of the population lives. Another trick to occupy journalists was looking straight at me, so I decided to sleep in, skip the bus trip to nowhere, and let others count the grains of desert sand. I decided to walk around Tripoli that same day and meet with Italian and French diplomats, arrangements I had made a day earlier. No one was left on the ship to notice when I skipped away near noon. No people or cars posing as taxis were visible on the streets either.

Libya was an Italian colony from 1911 until 1943. In 1989, Italy retained a kind of most-favored-nation status with Qaddafi's Libya. One benefit of that relationship was that the Italian embassy was near the El Kabir Hotel (The Grand Hotel), walking distance from Room 119 in the ship I called home. The Italians were friendlier than the Libyans, and happy to learn that an American journalist knew they were still in town.

The Italian diplomat I interviewed understood Qaddafi well: his swelling pragmatism would continue only until it clashed with his ideology, the diplomat told me. My long interview with Rome's emissaries finished, I thumbed a ride to the French embassy in the more distant Galgaresh diplomatic district. Exactly where that was I didn't know. But I knew it was way too far to walk. I also knew an Italian would be too friendly to turn down the urgency of my plea for a hitch in time to reach my French connection. Diplomatic relations aside, the distance between the Italian and French embassies told me that Qaddafi liked pasta better than quiche. French diplomats also proved helpful, free to talk about Qaddafi's Middle East policies partly because of the winding down of Libya's conflict with neighboring Chad, where French interests remained strong. To Libya's south and just as much a desert, Chad had been part of the French colonial empire from 1900 until 1960.

After I said *merci et au revoir* to my French hosts, I walked to the curb in a neighborhood I knew as well as I knew the back streets of Shanghai, which means not at all. No cars and no people greeted me. Even in which direction I should head to reach Room 119 wasn't immediately clear, although I could probably have figured that out before dawn. When a car approached after a long wait, I waved, my version of hitching under the circumstances. Right away I recognized the driver. He belonged to Qaddafi's special security. He wasn't difficult to identify: young, dark glasses, a military presence. Further evidence came in a flash as we drove through the vacant city streets at more than a hundred miles an hour. No flashing amber lights, no green or red lights either, no fear of being pulled over by the dictator's cops; my driver *was* a cop. After a pleasant but meaningless conversation, I was dropped off at the ship I called home. Too early to return to Room 119, I walked to the El Kabir Hotel, which was much closer than the French embassy. At the El Kabir, I enjoyed the magnificent Mediterranean equivalent of a New England Shore Dinner.

In the late afternoon, I strolled back to Room 119. The buses that set out hours earlier to find the invisible Great Man-Made River Project had returned and disgorged their disappointed and sleepy passengers.

"What did you see?" I asked two of the searchers.

"Nothing. You didn't miss anything," they answered.

I revealed nothing about what I'd learned from the Italian and French diplomats, or about hitching and whizzing at a hundred-miles-per hour through the streets of Tripoli after being lost in the diplomatic quarter.

Great Man-Made River Project, 1980s.
Photo: Jaap Berk Public Domain

SLOVENIA
*Ljubljana
CROATIA
*Belgrade
BOSNIA &
HERZEGOVINA
SERBIA
*
Pristina
KOSOVO
*Blace
*Skopje
MACEDONIA
ALBANIA

5 | A VISA HITCH TO KOSOVO

Hitching in the Balkans doesn't top my list of must-do activities in that fractious region of twisting mountains and querulous clans. Albanian, Greek, Turkish, and various Slavic factions, in all a combination of religious ticks, often show their love for each other by squeezing triggers and hurling bombs and ungodly insults. But sometimes hitching is necessary, even in more peaceful places.

To reach the small country of Macedonia, my destination in the heart of the Balkans, I booked a flight with a Macedonian airline that had no planes of its own. That Macedonian airline arranged for me to fly on a Russian-made jet that was operated by a Bulgarian airline. Those travel plans proved to be better than they looked, but the future was darker. Stormy weather delayed me in Ljubljana, the capital of Slovenia, a pleasant Slavic country on the northern edge of the Balkans and the southern edge of Austria. Overnight in Ljubljana was a delight, but I remained more than a ninety-minute flight from my destination, Skopje, Macedonia's capital. Though far from discouraged, I should have seen signs of a serious hitch in my travel plans.

Ringed by mountains, Skopje is warm by day but much cooler at night. The city of more than a million was also crippled by the hostilities among surrounding clans. Western Europe, the United Nations, and the United States feared the Bosnian wars would seek more oxygen by seeping into Macedonia, notably from neighboring Serbia. The name Macedonia alone was troublesome. When I first entered the country in mid-May of 1994, Macedonia was known by its United Nations designation as FYROM, or the Former Yugoslav Republic of Macedonia, a catchy tune. One point of that acronym, which missed its mark, was to quiet Greece. FYROM was a bit cumbersome as a moniker for the new nation formed in 1991, when it split from Yugoslavia. Since 2019 it's been known as the Republic of North Macedonia, a more acceptable name in the region, especially to Greece.

When I landed in Skopje, Macedonia's political problem was as much historical and geographical as contemporary. Parts of Greece and Bulgaria share the label of Macedonia. But Greece alone strongly objected to FYROM, seeing that name as usurping the name Macedonia from the Greeks of Philip and his son Alexander the Great's moment in history more than two thousand years earlier. The new FYROM also pasted the blazing Vergina Sun on its new flag. Greece considers the sun burst to be *its* national symbol. History and national emotions aside, it's easy to see that the dispute over FYROM's name and flag was irrational, more one of nationalism run amok, as no one could possibly confuse Greece and Athens with FYROM and Skopje. FYROM solved the problem by becoming the Republic of North Macedonia and changing the sunburst on its flag to a single blazing star radiating in all directions.

One village near Skopje sports a Macedonian name, a Serbian name, and an Albanian name. Take your pick. That alone reflected part of the new country's ethnic problems. In the spring of 1994, Macedonia had a substantial Albanian population. In theory ethnic Albanians signaled trouble for Macedonia's Slavic majority. Serbia and Kosovo hovered to the north of the new Macedonia, or FYROM. Serbia was a main provocateur of the war in Bosnia-Herzegovina and Croatia. Though ninety percent Albanian and then a province of Serbia, Kosovo was suppressed by Serbia and seething with resentment. The Albanian uprising in Serbia's Kosovo was less than four years in the future. Albania itself, on the new Macedonia's western border, was three years away from the chaotic raids on its military bases and police barracks that would result in fresh weapons ending up in the hands of the Albanians in Kosovo.

Nervous Western powers feared that Serbia would attempt to widen the war in Bosnia by invading Macedonia and disrupting social, economic and political life there. Macedonia had, at most, 10,000 soldiers in uniform and 2,000 officers. They were equipped with only machine guns, and "maybe four mortars," the top American commander there told me. The Macedonian army had no armor or heavy artillery, five fixed-wing aircraft but no fuel, and two police helicopters but no jets. The country's population was just under two million at the time. In its first-ever mission to prevent conflict, the United Nations stepped into the breach to protect Macedonia from internal strife between Albanians and Slavs, and to prevent the Bosnian war from bleeding into the country. The UN soldiers totaled almost 1,100. Just over 500 members of that UN force came from the United States, a rare occasion when American soldiers came under UN command. The U.S. presence was called Operation Able Sentry. Its mission was warily simple, to observe, detect, and ward off trouble from Serbia, firing only in self-defense.

As I hitched my way around what was then called the Former Yugoslav Republic of Macedonia, I found its political and religious leaders welcoming the Americans as "saviors" for simply doing a peacekeeping job. The small American camp overlooking the border with Serbia had beautiful mountain views, but little else. No overt tension hovered over the misty peaks and valleys when I bummed through the area. Most of the time, the military task was boring, but the possibility of provocation was so ever-present that high-powered glasses were always trained across the border. Only a dozen American soldiers were assigned to watch for unusual military activity a few yards away. By this time, Serbian leaders had received the message: don't provoke the American or the UN forces, which in this case were the same. Peace prevailed at the Macedonian-Serbian border.

The glue that held Macedonia together and brought help from the UN and the West was its seventy-six-year-old president Kiro Gligorov. American and international commanders and diplomats all told me that Gligorov deserved their trust at that explosive moment. A strong and committed personality, Gligorov never stopped evolving, first from a Slavic nationalist and supporter of a pan-Slavic Yugoslavia to a Macedonian patriot, then from a Communist to a free-market democrat. Born in 1917 during World War I, in a small city in the country's east, Gligorov was a devoted Macedonian his entire life. He descended from a family that had fought against the long domination of the Ottoman Turks. As Hitler's Nazi empire swept across Europe in the late 1930s and early 1940s, Gligorov joined the anti-fascist resistance. He went on to play a leading role when, in 1944, Macedonia joined five other Balkan states to form Yugoslavia.

Throughout most of Yugoslavia's nearly fifty-year existence, Gligorov held several important positions in the country's federal government. He joined the Yugoslav Communist Party in 1944, but later led the way toward market-based economic reforms against strong opposition and condemnation from within. In the 1980s, his focus shifted back toward Macedonia where he began advocating democratic reforms and western models of independent institutions within a strong legal system, a multi-party system, and a market economy. When Yugoslavia imploded in 1991, Macedonia was ready for independence because Gligorov had laid the foundation. Shortly after the people voted for independence in 1991, they elected Gligorov as the country's founding president. He was re-elected four years later, and he served until his second term expired in 1999. When he left office, Gligorov was the oldest serving president of any nation. He died at age 94, on January 1, 2012.

Early in October, 1995, Gligorov was severely injured in an assassination attempt. He lost an arm and the sight in his right eye. His driver was killed in the bomb attack, his bodyguard and several bystanders were injured. The crime has not been solved.

When I interviewed Gligorov in his presidential office fifteen months before the attempt on his life, I quickly learned why he was so respected by insiders and outsiders. Of the many political, military, diplomatic, princely, and revolutionary leaders I've interviewed over the years, Gligorov was equal to any, and he surpassed most. He backed up his plea for international help with specific requests for protection against outside forces and for economic and financial aid to bolster the country internally. Trim and with a full head of salt and pepper hair, he looked a decade younger than his seventy-six years when he told me the international community had a "moral obligation" to help Macedonia survive economically and to "maintain its peace and stability." He appealed along intellectual and moral grounds, not like a man begging from his knees.

The Balkans, specifically Serbia, Croatia, and Bosnia-Herzegovina, were still embroiled in war when I spoke with

Gligorov through an interpreter for more than an hour. He pleaded for his country's survival as a democratic republic, and I wanted to listen and tell the world his story.

Gligorov led Macedonia to break with Yugoslavia in 1991, as the Bosnian wars began. Macedonia avoided the war, and he wanted to remain on its sidelines. Other European nations, along with the United States, were helping Gligorov and protecting Macedonia from becoming prey of other nations in the Balkans. Pleading for diplomatic, economic, and military help to ensure his country's survival and growth, his was a full-time job.

Gligorov proudly waved his true colors as a patriot and a liberal nationalist. Next to his desk, along with a television set that connected him to world news, a Macedonian flag stood at anchor. Behind his desk was a large tableau of individual Orthodox Christian icons blended to form one picture. A large painting of the 1903 Macedonian uprising against the Ottoman Turks hung on a wall of his office. Gligorov wasn't anti other nations, but he worried that the influential "Greek lobby" in the United States would prevent Washington from installing an ambassador in Skopje. At the time, the American mission in Skopje was described as a liaison office, although a large circular sign in that office said "Embassy United States of America" with a golden eagle and an American flag. Full embassy status was at hand. Gligorov had gotten through to President Bill Clinton's Washington. All he said about his antagonists at the time was that the Greek embargo against Macedonia and economic sanctions against warring Serbia were harming Macedonia. The large Albanian population in Macedonia worried Gligorov because of the explosive potential in neighboring Kosovo, which was about ninety percent Albanian and oppressed by Serbia.

The road signs on my story map all pointed to Kosovo. How to get there was my puzzle to solve. Until this moment, I'd been unable to get a Yugoslav visa, and I'd tried in capitals on three continents. The simplest approach often works best, and it did again. With Arzim as a guide, I decided to head directly to the border crossing at Blacë, where Macedonia and Kosovo touch. There I would act like I belonged, ask for a visa, and get it.

Arzim and I had met at the Grand Hotel (where else?) in Skopje. An ethnic-Albanian who knew his way around journalism, Arzim arranged for the transportation: a friend who had a car, always a good way to bum a ride. One pleasant afternoon we rode to the border with Kosovo. I had money and my wits. Arzim had the lingo and his calmness. The line of trucks and cars was longer than long, but we sidestepped all that rubber and metal. We left Arzim's friend where the exhaust pipes ended and strolled casually all the way to the border post. Arzim would do the talking. I would advise if troublesome questions arose. None did. My instructions to Arzim were simple. Tell the truth. Say that I'm an American journalist who wanted a visa to visit Kosovo. Arzim complied. So did the Serbians at Blacë. Arzim and I received Yugoslav (Serbian, really) visas that were valid for seven days. No charge. The next time I received a Yugoslav visa was in Sofia, Bulgaria, almost three years later. There I paid a secret middleman $100.

Once past the border, Kosovo's soil was beneath my boots, but I was stuck. The road to Kosovo's capital lay ahead. My destination, Kosovo's capital Pristina, was where I would gauge the tinderbox that was Kosovo. Adem Demaci, known as the Albanian Mandela for the nearly three decades he was silenced in a Serbian/Yugoslav prison, lived in the capital. The Serbian killer nicknamed Arkan had holed up there. A branch of Mother

Teresa's minions was planted in Pristina. My immediate need was a ride, another car.

Arzim and I walked quickly away from the border. We didn't run because we didn't want it to appear that we were fleeing from anything or too eager to go where we shouldn't. But we wanted to get out of sight before the border police remembered the full meaning of the word journalist. Hilly farm country surrounded us, where horses, cows, and what looked to me like water buffalo far outnumbered people. A half-hour later, we reached a road, the only one in the area that led to Pristina. We flagged cars, hitching with our waving arms rather than thumbs, and finally one stopped. An old man asked Arzim our intentions.

"Pristina, where else?" Arzim answered.

When we landed in Pristina about an hour later, I paid the driver a few dollars for the lift and started searching for Arkan, whose real name was Zeljko Raznatovic. We never found Arkan, a certified killer. For a week Arzim and I lived in the battered, wretched hotel that Arkan once called home. We camped in the only room that was suitable for humans rather than for roaches and rats.

Wobbling around Pristina proved easy. Many people of all stripes wanted to tell the story of Serbian oppression against Albanians.

One human rights worker led to a half dozen others. Before long, another driver whom Arzim and I had flagged led me to the greatest and longest-suffering Albanian of them all, a gentle man tagged with the great but sad honor of being called the Albanian Mandela.

When I knocked on Adem Demaci's door, I expected a large and angry man to turn the knob. Serenity greeted me instead. Calm, small and dapper, Demaci had been the historical and intellectual leader of Kosovo's Albanian population for decades. His presence was felt although he had long been removed from Pristina's streets. For waving an Albanian flag, writing graffiti, and uttering nationalistic slogans in public places, Demaci had spent twenty-eight of his fifty-eight years in prison. All he wanted was equal rights for the huge Albanian population in Kosovo. All the Serbian-led Yugoslav government wanted was to suppress the Albanians or drive them out. When he wasn't living in "cold, dark, dirty places" with "madmen and criminals of the most hardened kind," Demaci languished alone. Five and-a half years of his prison time were spent in solitary confinement. He supped on the thinnest of gruel with walls as companions. His thoughts alone taught him that serenity was the path to personal survival. Demaci was aptly known as the Albanian Mandela, not only because of the long and wildly unjust prison terms they both served, but because inner strength powered the survival of both. I never met Nelson Mandela, but I've come to learn how he coped with imprisonment by burying his hate and relying on his calmness and strong mind to overcome his adversaries. Demaci did the same.

Demaci wouldn't take up arms to lead the revolution. That wasn't his persona. But he knew conditions existed to ignite an upheaval. A writer by profession, he was president of Kosovo's human rights council and editor of a magazine that couldn't be published because its coffers were empty. What the Serbs wanted, ethnic cleansing, was clearer than ever to Demaci at the moment we talked. The Serbs wanted to move the Albanians out of Kosovo and to replace them with Serbs. That meant rebellion. Weapons obtained from ransacked barracks in Albania itself came later. Then came the rebellion. Several health and human rights organizations reiterated Demaci's concerns. They were all correct; only the Serbs were wrong. The Kosovo Liberation Army emerged in 1996. The Albanian uprising against Serbian domination began in 1998. After intense fighting followed by NATO's intervention, Kosovo declared its independence in 2008. Yugoslavia vanished when Montenegro split with Serbia in 2006.

In 1997, Arkan was indicted for war crimes by the United Nations International War Crimes Tribunal in The Hague. In the year 2000, at age forty-seven, Arkan fell to a hail of gunfire in the lobby of a hotel in Belgrade, Serbia. Arkan's killers delivered his form of justice.

Adem Damaci died a natural death in 2018 at age eighty-two. He lived to see a free and independent Kosovo, a reward for his lifelong hardships and time served.

Hitching, flagging cars, begging, thumbing, even walking are unbeatable ways to learn what reason says I might not have found out in more conventional ways. As Arzim and I took the road from Pristina back to Macedonia, I thought of my hike across Athens, from Mt. Lycabettus past the Acropolis all the way to the port of Piraeus, a good fifteen miles. That's a leisurely four- or five-hour walk, depending on one's pace and age. It took much longer on a sultry Sunday in May when I plucked oranges from roadside trees and chatted with Greeks along the way. Pointing to my head, locals asked whether I was ill and wondered why I was taking a walk they avoided.

I learned more about Greeks and Turks on the sidewalks of Athens and Istanbul than I did in palaces and at state functions. Lessons like that informed my life on the road.

Leaving Adem Damaci and Pristina proved easier than entering. I didn't need another visa to return to Macedonia. All I needed was a car. Arms waving again, Arzim and I hooked a driver. An hour later, we left Kosovo behind. We were within walking distance of the Blacë border post, among the same hills and trees where, a week earlier, we had hitched to Pristina. The same old cows, horses, and water buffalo decorated the land.

A soldierly American woman looked down from a tower on British and Canadian men in uniform; all were on duty checking the work of Macedonian customs officials. The three observers applied a light touch at the border. They were part of three teams of international customs checkers, unarmed civilian police and customs monitors whose combined presence was to prevent conflict among Serbs, Macedonians and Albanians. Eager to leave the border behind, I had missed all this activity earlier when Kosovo beckoned. My slower exit revealed the subtle activity I had missed. The activities of Macedonian customs officers puzzled the UN officials at Blacë. Why, the officials wondered, did the Macedonians hold up cars and trucks for hours at the border before opening the floodgates and letting every vehicle flow through? The answers rested in the Serbian/Croatian/Bosnian war that raged in the Balkans, the war in Kosovo rising on the horizon, and Macedonia's future as a civil society. The lesson for me was, as always, get off my arse and see things for myself.

Leaving Blacë, I waved at the soldiers. No one noticed. At the end of the long line pointing toward Kosovo, Arzim and I hailed a car and pointed in the direction of Skopje. Within two hours, we were at the Grand Hotel. Where else?

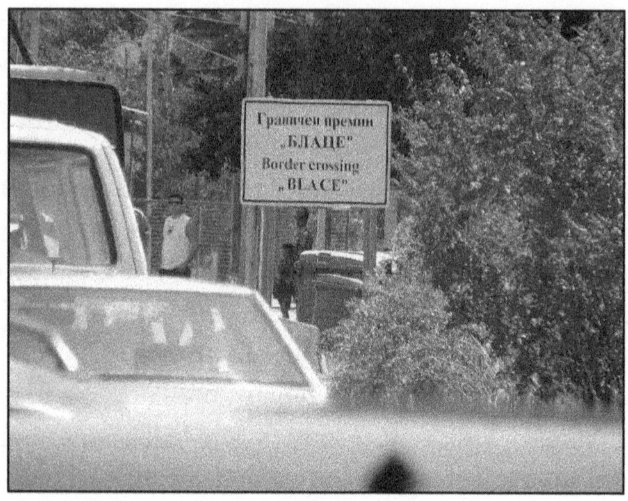

Blace Border Crossing between Macedonia and Kosovo
Photo: David Bailey, CC BY-SA 2.0

Mural_of_Željko_Ražnatović_Arkan, Belgrade
Photo: Public Domain

Grand Hotel Skopje. Photo: Public Domain

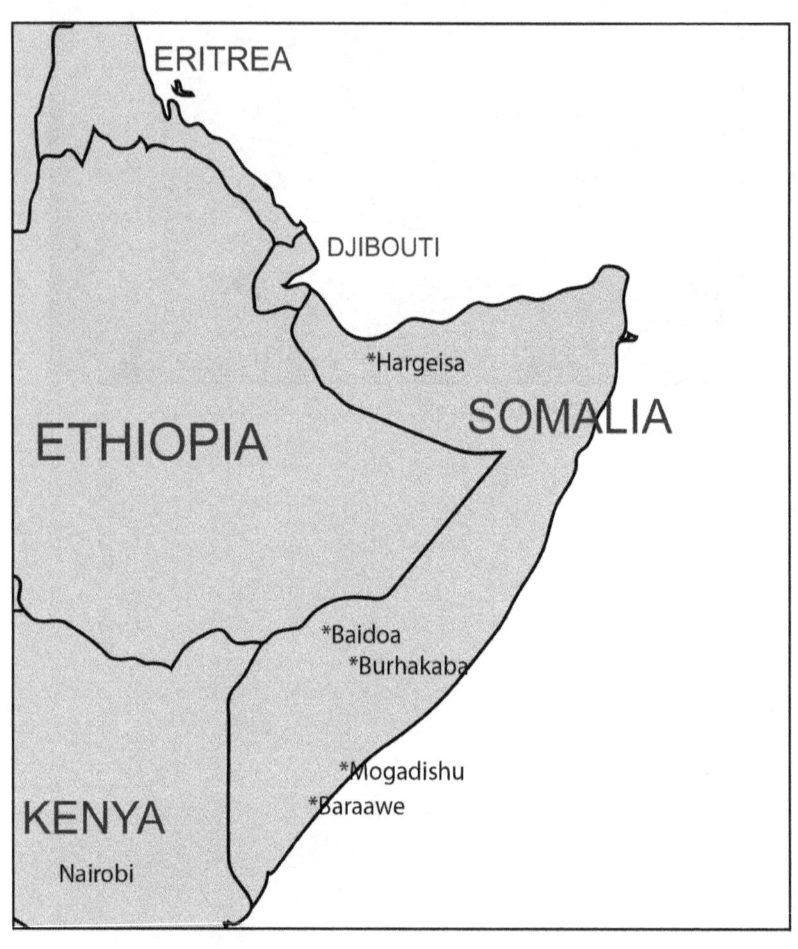
ERITREA
DJIBOUTI
*Hargeisa
SOMALIA
ETHIOPIA
*Baidoa
*Burhakaba
*Mogadishu
*Baraawe
KENYA
Nairobi

6 | WITH HERCULES IN SOMALIA

With seven other passengers on a nine-passenger Beechcraft, I hitched from Nairobi, Kenya, to Mogadishu, Somalia, to chronicle the lingering death of a state and its people in the early nineties. The two and a half hour United Nations flight over East Africa passed without drama. What followed was beyond drama: it was brutal reality, more sadness shrouding unrelenting starvation and death than I had ever witnessed or thought possible. Reporting in Somalia was difficult due to the devastating pain and heartache I couldn't avoid. My work was important to Somalis and the world, I felt, but I was only passing through. I would hitch, witness, report and leave. Too many Somalis never left, or would leave only when they died. They were departing the land of the living in numbers too great for me or anyone else to count.

The bare landing zone alone tipped me off to the horrors of drought, famine, and war. Colonies of partially built or falling down houses rose to the lip of battered asphalt called a runway. Countless broken appliances lined the landing strip, a junkyard of rusting metal. We drove into the city in ordinary UN vehicles dressed up with machine guns and armed guards weighed down with ammo. Dirt kicked up beneath our tires because we took a ragged lower road for better protection. The upper road, though paved, was an open target and too dangerous. Our drive into the capital told the human story. Sheets of plastic covering twigs and cardboard were called houses: but lean-tos would have been a more accurate description. A few camels, once called herds, small white goats and stunted corn stalks caught my eye. This was not the scenic route.

In the days that followed, I rode in many more armed vehicles and hitched on other flights throughout that sad land. Wherever I traveled, in the capital city and hundreds of miles into the bush country, I saw firsthand an unfathomable depth of suffering. Women, children and old people died from hunger alone. Medicine was even harder to find than food. What food was brought in by sea or air couldn't be protected or distributed. Much of it was stolen by competing clan warlords and used as a weapon of war. Experienced humanitarian workers said conditions in Somalia were worse than any they had ever seen. This wasn't all Somalia's fault. Its eastern elbow sticking out strategically on the Horn of Africa, Somalia was a battleground in the Cold War. Weapons from arms manufacturers the world over filled the country. Those weapons weren't hard to find long after the Cold War warriors had vanished. Somalis turned those weapons, brought in by others, on themselves when the Cold War ended.

Well before I reached it, Somalia was described as a failed state. More than three decades later it remains so, having been joined more recently by Yemen and Syria, where war's destructive effects live on. With famine and drought added to war, Somalia retains its pathetic advantage, although war alone usually leads to hunger and sometimes starvation. States fail when they are unable to provide basic human needs, when organized economies collapse, crime and corruption rule, and food security exists elsewhere.

My roof in Mogadishu was a house owned by the former finance minister in the regime of Somalia's previous dictator,

Mohammed Siad Barre, who died in 1995 in Nigeria, Africa's far west. The finance minister was living comfortably in Italy when I called his house my home. The UN rented the house because there was no other safe choice. I paid the UN a small fee for safety. Deep in the bush country I was offered a long, dark cave for survival. I declined the offer. In the capital city, warning signs, spoken and written, were everywhere: Everyone has a gun. Don't go out without armed guards. If you're told not to take photos, don't take photos. If you're asked for cash to cross from one clan-controlled area to another, pay up. Somalis were dying. Following a few simple rules seemed prudent so I wouldn't add to the numbers.

My thumb was useless. Packs of American cigarettes, such as those I flashed to stop taxis in Moscow, would have been useless, too. Traffic in Somalia's capital was limited to vehicles armed by others and unsafe for strangers. Roads themselves were unsafe. The few traffic signals that posed as signs of law and order did little to abide their purpose. Most traffic signals didn't even blink. Only by air was hitching possible. As I hitched on a plane to enter the country, I would later hitch on planes to enter Somalia's far north and west, and, finally, to quit the country for Nairobi.

In the meantime, my choice was simple: hook up with a "technical," a fully armed and specially equipped Toyota Land Cruiser, or a pick-up similarly armed; or go home. I didn't enter Somalia to leave without bearing witness and telling the world. A half-dozen family members and friends came with each "technical." The cars and pickups weren't sophisticated. They were equipped, however, to survive one-hundred-and-fifty mile trips into the bush country, to outwit flawed fuel systems, to limp home after striking a goat, and to scare off thieves. After a

UN worker warned against taking a step outside the compound without armed guards, I hired my very own "technical."

On day trips throughout the capital, I visited a hospital with little medicine, food stations with insufficient food to prevent a dozen people from dying each night, and the seaport where too little food was shipped in to feed the dying. What food entered the country couldn't be distributed safely or was stolen.

"We had people come into our office with a grenade in their hands and the pin pulled out saying, 'Where is our food?'" a humanitarian worker told me.

Medina Hospital had only twenty beds. Tents outside held sixty more beds. Doctors said most people died from bullet wounds and thirty percent of those died from a lack of blood for transfusions. One eight-year-old boy hung around the hospital looking for food. The boy's right leg had been amputated, and his entire family except for a grandmother had been killed in the civil war.

"It's a country totally devastated. There's nothing," a UN representative told me. "The only commodity available in Somalia are guns," he said. I saw nothing to refute that view.

Conditions were even worse outside the capital where drought and famine struck the hardest. The pipeline of devastation that led starving people to flee from the bush country to villages and cities in search of food worsened conditions throughout the country. One agency reported that it was bringing in 20,000 tons of food each month and "needed to double that amount to make a difference."

A representative of the International Committee of the Red Cross said, "We are desperately looking for an improvement in the security situation so we can get more food in and distribute it properly."

Nowhere – not in Bosnia, isolated Nagorno-Karabakh in the South Caucasus, or Afghanistan – did I feel as much an intruder as in Somalia. To people trying to eke out another day by eating insects and chewing on strips of rawhide, I must have looked like a naked voyeur. At times it seemed as if I were standing guard over fresh graves. My intention, of course, was to save Somalia by telling the world why the country and its people were dying. Somalis themselves wanted water and food, not a journalist gawking at and photographing them, and filing words and pictures they couldn't eat and would never see. Clan leaders wanted to fight for power without interference from outsiders so they could continue to profit from the catastrophe. Somali chiefs didn't want me, others like me, or foreign powers to change the rules. Only foreign agencies trying to rescue the country from the ravages of Somalia's own apocalyptic present enlisted help from other outsiders. I'm not whining about the difficulties of reporting from Somalia, only noting the contradictions that built barriers.

My "technical," a pick-up this time, was ready. With me were a driver, translator, and four gunmen riding in the truck bed along with a "friend of the family." I didn't argue, and we got along. Drought and famine were deeper in Baidoa, I was told. Not enough food reached that city to keep enough people from the burying ground. Baidoa's population was elastic, floating between 60,000 and 100,000, depending on the shifting number of migrants seeking food who flowed in from villages deeper in the bush country. With the name of a UN agent tucked in my shirt pocket, I wouldn't be alone in Baidoa.

More than one-hundred and fifty miles and slightly northwest of the capital, Baidoa beckoned. Asphalt wound from Mogadishu to my destination, but the road was a ribbon through bandit country. Crossing from one clan's fiefdom to another required a special pass and cash. I had both, but the gunman at the checkpoint wanted more cash. I refused to double the fare, handed over a five-dollar tip, declared the guard a winner, and moved on. No one was gunned down.

More than halfway into the nearly four-hour drive we hit trouble in Burhakaba, a village tucked around a huge monolith. Before I realized what was happening, my gunmen threw fists full of local cash into the air and sped through the village; I would have called it burning rubber in my college days. Before it was too late, I contributed my share of filthy lucre to occupy the villagers. This was another moment when trusting friends I met on the road paid life-saving dividends. Big trouble might have ensued had not my protectors, in a flash, sensed the problem. Villagers were desperate for food but I, and all my possessions, would have sufficed.

The Welcome Wagon didn't show when I entered Baidoa.

"There's a cave near here where you can stay," George said. "You'll be safe if you sleep in the back. All the other people there will sleep in front." George, a UN worker, was the man I was looking for. He was my contact, the man who would explain Baidoa's desperation. Our relationship improved quickly.

"I'm not staying there," I told George. "Do you have an office?"

"Yes," George answered.

"OK, I'll sleep in a chair at your desk." We went to George's office. George left and returned with a cot, a camper's version. That was my bed in Baidoa. The common shower, a pail of water above my head and a rope to pull on and unleash the water, was outside. For dinner on that first night, George took me to a soup kitchen so he and I could avoid a racial spat among the mix of humanitarian workers. Soup, I knew, would bring me to my knees immediately, so I passed on the soup.

In Baidoa, the war had ended. But the rains didn't come, crops shriveled, and people starved. Locals ate seeds rather than plant them, a short-term solution, but deadly long-term. Even the large camel herds were killed and eaten, long gone by the time I arrived.

"This place makes Mogadishu look like Nairobi," one worker said.

Another aid worker said the villages outside were so woeful they made Baidoa look like Paris. Baidoa was like no other place I'd ever seen.

An estimated 50,000 Somali civilians were killed during the three-and-a-half years of civil war that had left drought, famine, and food warfare still alive. When I reached the bush country, Somalis had been dying of hunger for two years. Baidoa introduced me to the limits of what humans can endure and, if they're lucky, survive. In that mix were the courage and dedication of humanitarian workers who tried desperately to feed the starving, heal the wounded, and clothe the semi-naked. Scenes were so primitive that desperate, helpless people carried cans or strips of cloth on the off-chance that they would find bits of food to collect and turn into a meal. People were so malnourished, nurses said, that no matter what illness they got, it would be fatal. The International Committee of the Red Cross served beans and rice from large barrels cut in half that were used as pots. A Red Cross feeding center was at an old army base, with four anti-aircraft guns in the yard and one on the roof, each inoperable. Twenty-two Red Cross food kitchens in the area each fed 1,500 people a day. That wasn't nearly enough as thousands of people drifted into Baidoa from far-off villages.

After several days reporting in Baidoa, I could leave. Somalis dying there could not. The humanitarian workers stayed on. It didn't take long to gather my gunmen for the long drive back to Mogadishu. Trouble rode with us. It wasn't long before my team became high while chewing the local narcotic leaf known as Qat or Chat. Chew a little Chat and you either fall asleep or become wildly giddy. Fortunately, our driver didn't fall asleep, but he did become so happy and out of control that we struck and killed a goat, an irreplaceable source of wealth and food in the bush country. Hitting a goat snapped my crew to attention. Quicker than we could say Qat, we paid for the goat and settled our differences with the goat's owner, reaching an essential truce. The goat had wiped out the left headlight and badly damaged the fender and grill. We limped back to Mogadishu, a wobbly spare tire in place but without further trouble.

With the pick-up out of commission, I was forced to bum or beg for a more reliable "technical." My objective was Baraave on Somalia's south coast. My new transport was another victim of hard times. Though it was a Land Cruiser, with a driver and three armed guards, it also labored under false pretenses because it came with a dead battery, no ignition and a jerry-rigged fuel system that required tinkering with a large plastic container of diesel fuel under the hood. How I longed for my Fifty Ford, flawed flywheel, leaky master cylinder, and all. A tank of Somali diesel fuel cost a mere 780,000 Somali shillings, or $110, a bit pricey for a vehicle that wouldn't get close to where I was headed. To start the Land Cruiser, the driver touched two wires under the steering column; sometimes we pushed the car. Bouncing along on a dirt road, we lost the rear-view mirror on the driver's side as the spare tire bounced from the car's roof to the dirt. Cows and goats stumbled along the road in this relatively fertile area of cornfields and banana trees.

The country had collapsed to the extent that the food in this area couldn't be harvested, while drought brought famine deeper inland. We hadn't traveled halfway to the port city of Baraawe when it became clear to all, especially to me, that we wouldn't complete the one hundred- and twelve-mile journey. Frustrated, my team and I reversed direction, a day wasted but I was richer in hitching experience and with no goat-owner to pay off. Patching and repairing what we could, stumbling back to Mogadishu was our only choice.

Hitching, sometimes risky and always stimulating enough to keep me fully conscious, added a new twist in Somalia. It was vital and fascinating beyond expectations. What turned into hitching on a wing and by luck began when a handful of serious looking men who weren't dying gathered outside the UN house. Eavesdropping at the edge of the conversations, I overheard one of the men say that a small plane was heading to a place worse than Baidoa and deeper into the bush country. No more "technicals" for me, I thought. At that moment, but not for the first time, I realized that eavesdropping followed by hitching opened more doors than if I had flown my own helicopter.

A twin-engine propeller-driven aircraft, small enough to land in an unmarked space in the desert, was my ticket to Bardhere, more than 200 air miles from Mogadishu. I went along for the ride engineered by Giovanni Bersani, an Italian senator with an abiding interest in helping Somalia. Bersani was no junketeer. Well past balding and almost eighty when we met, Bersani died in 2014, at age 100. His meeting with Somali leader Gen. Mohammed Farah Aideed at Aideed's compound just off the landing strip wasn't a photo op. Bersani was engaged in a serious attempt to help Somalia's weakest and poorest. Some 2,000 starving shepherds had drifted into town in the previous three days. Food was their objective. They badly missed their target, or their target eluded them. No roads led to Bardhere, only dusty trails over which shepherds tramped, begging for food that wasn't there.

Bersani wore the look of an old professor. His work in the Italian government focused on social welfare and labor issues. Italy had a lengthy colonial interest in Somalia, in what was called Italian Somaliland, but its influence in the country had waned to almost zero, although Bersani's zeal to help had not. Trying to quell the internal warfare and ensure that food reached the starving, Bersani was in his rightful personal space.

Good fortune landed me aboard Bersani's plane that skidded to a stop in the swirling dust near Bardhere. The senator met General Mohamed Farrah Aideed, and so did I. Aideed was a principal clan leader in South and Central Somalia. Bersani wanted to ensure that food sent into the country would be protected and used to feed the famished rather than used as a weapon of control by Aideed or competing clan chiefs. While Bersani and Aideed met privately, I talked to town elders.

"There's no looting here," one man told me through an interpreter. "There is nothing to loot." Food came in the form of grass, leaves and camel skin.

Educated in Moscow and Paris, Aideed was savvy. Swinging his trademark black cane with a silver top and tapping the cane in the dirt for emphasis, Aideed emerged from his meeting with Bersani with a plea and a warning. A handsome man, with typically fine Somali facial features, his hair graying on the sides and balding on top, Aideed said he'd allow the UN to train up to 6,000 Somali police. But he rejected the presence of UN troops in the country for any reason. Aideed said that he'd allow UN civilians only to observe the distribution of food. His meaning was clear: Aideed alone wanted to control what life-saving food entered the country and the power that went along with such control. No other clan leader need apply for that job in Aideed's territory.

Before sunset on that same day, Bersani, his small entourage, and I left Bardhere's destitution, thrilled that we could do so by air. At the same moment, thousands of others flocked into the town seeking food that wasn't there.

We flew back to Mogadishu, from where I was itching to fly north to Hargeisa, capital of a rump territory called Somaliland. Within a year, Aideed's forces killed twenty-four Pakistani UN troops who were aiming to silence Aideed's radio station. A short time after that, eighteen American soldiers fell to Aideed's clan. Eighty other Americans were wounded and three U.S. helicopters were brought down. Aideed escaped an abortive UN manhunt, but was killed during clan warfare in 1996, almost four years to the day when he tipped his cane in my direction. Today, some thirty years later, Somalia continues its plunge into what seems like a graveyard without measure.

Hunkering in a UN safe house was the perfect place to cadge a ride from Mogadishu north to Somaliland. Flying was just about the only way to reach Hargeisa, a dump of rusting Cold War era weapons. I didn't have a plane.

Within a few hours, I was aboard a Lockheed C-130 Hercules cargo plane whose distended belly made it look pregnant with baby planes. The Hercules is a huge aircraft. Its cavernous cargo hold is flexible enough to ferry more than 40,000 pounds of just about anything in any form, such as ninety combat troops, armored vehicles, or helicopters. Built to operate in rough terrain, the four-engine propeller driven Hercules was perfect for taking off and landing in Somalia's unmarked dirt. The pilot had no trouble rolling over broken asphalt and dodging sinkholes in Mogadishu's pathetic runway.

Strapped to the fuselage's innards so we wouldn't fly around the empty cargo cave, I, along with three other passengers and the flight crew, headed north. We were bound for Hargeisa. Our first stop, for a few hours overnight, was the former French colony of Djibouti, directly on the Horn of Africa. After a troublesome hitch at Djibouti's airport concerning my ancestry and passport, which I rescued after midnight from an abandoned airport office in the midst of serious renovation, Hercules and I bid adieu to Djibouti shortly after 4 a.m. the following day. We touched down on sand just east of Hargeisa, at another landing spot that did nothing to dignify the desert.

Ready to greet me in Hargeisa was the first president of the Republic of Somaliland, none other than Abdirahman Ahmed Ali Tuur. This isn't the way it sounds. Tuur didn't expect me, and I didn't expect to meet him. He didn't know I would hitch a ride on a UN plane. He surely didn't figure I'd hitch my way to his veranda and a meeting with a bevy of UN officials.

But there I was, so Tuur and I talked about the past, present and future of Somaliland (a former British colony) and the rest of Somalia (a former Italian colony). Tuur wore brown sandals and red-checkered pants, and a shawl over his left shoulder touched a beige robe trimmed in maroon. He spoke softly through a gravelly voice, a good impersonation of Marlon Brando's Godfather, I thought. As Tuur explained the roots of Somalia's long civil war and his opposition to the Somali dictator, Mohammed Siad Barre, who ruled from 1969 to 1991, Somalia's contradictions became clearer. Like Aideed in the south, Tuur appealed for foreign aid and temporary, unarmed, observers, but not foreign soldiers to enforce a tribal peace. He opposed the reunification of the country, north and south. The only way to disarm the "young boys," he said, "is to have enough food for them, and the government didn't have enough food."

Besides rivalries within his own party, Tuur pointed to another problem that he could do nothing about. Qat, or Chat, the narcotic leaf, he said, was another enemy of Somaliland. Many people begin chewing Chat at 1:30 each afternoon and are supposed to resume work at 4:30, but few do. One aide worker said that chewing Chat "is a national problem, and any serious discussions are done under its influence. It's out of control, a national addiction."

"It's remarkably peaceful here," the UNICEF director in the area told me. Those words were relative. Yes, the UN official confessed, his car was looted at the local landing strip, and it was stolen, but what shooting there was, was mostly random.

Mohammed Warsami, the UN coordinator of Non-Government Organizations in the region, told me, "There's no big hunger problem here. The economy works here. I can't explain how it works, but it does."

Fighting among clans was over. The civil war had drained everyone's zeal for more blood. The director of Save the Children in the region, John Battery, said, "We're not in a situation of acute malnutrition distress here, but very little works here in terms of government services. There's some health service, and schools are working, but many people, maybe 80,000 to 90,000, have fled to Ethiopia," itself no safe haven from human misery. The UN's objective was a tall order: to import by land, sea and air some 35,000 tons of food each month, or more than 400,000 tons a year until Somalis could resume growing their own food.

Taking no chances in the midst of sporadic fighting and consistent uncertainty, Tuur moved his wife and family to London. In his early sixties when we talked, Tuur rested in the middle of a two-year term as president. Tuur promised that he would leave office after his term ended, and he did. He walked into the sunset in 1993. He died in 2003, at age 72, in London.

I left Somaliland earlier than Tuur. A couple of thousand people, most shouting and screaming good wishes, gathered around the mighty but still-empty Hercules as we boarded the plane. We could have airlifted a couple of hundred weary Somalis with us, but that would have upset hundreds more. The same four passengers and crew that landed near Hargeisa lifted off, bound for Mogadishu. I was thrilled that we skirted Djibouti. Strapped once more to the fuselage of the plane so we didn't knock ourselves out in the otherwise empty cavern, we took off without blowing a tire or running over a friend. Somehow, we landed with fully inflated tires. It wasn't long before I bummed another UN flight to Nairobi. Two more flights, a couple of days later, took me first to Athens and then to my home base in Jerusalem. Far behind me were Somalis and their fractured land, where famine and factionalism continue to this day, three decades after what were supposed to be their worst of times.

Lockheed Hercules C-130. Photo: Public Domain

A Somali "Technical"
Wikipedia: CT Snow from Hsinchu, Taiwan

Italian Senator Giovanni Bersani.
Photo: Public Domain

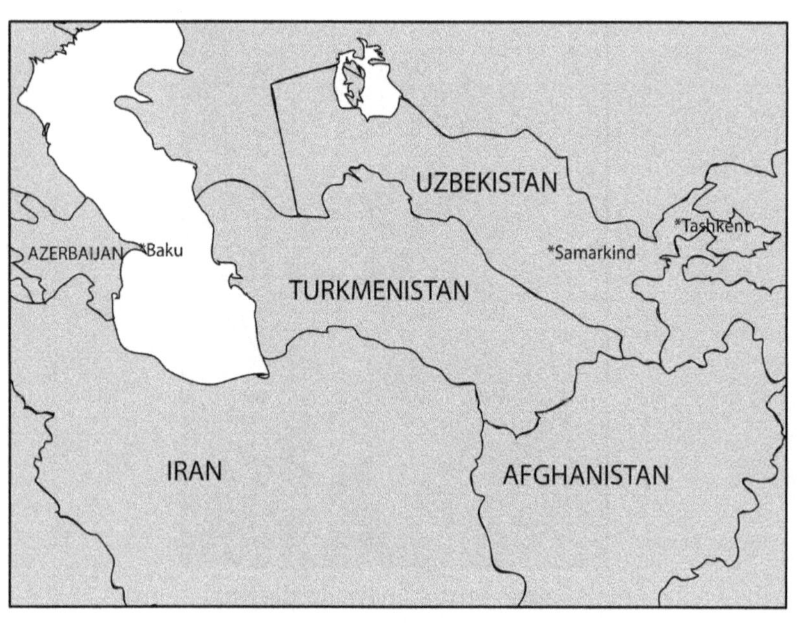
UZBEKISTAN
*Tashkent
AZERBAIJAN
*Baku
*Samarkind
TURKMENISTAN
IRAN
AFGHANISTAN

7 | RACING WITH A GRENADE

Tamar acted like an All American boy. Except for time, place, car, and uniform, he could have been Rudy, my mechanical genius back in Millville in 1960. Tamar had personally engineered his tan Russian-made Moskvitch sedan to fly through the post-Soviet Wild East. If Tamar became bored on our long drives, he flipped on a tape of top twenty hits from the fifties and sixties, further evidence of the universal power of American pop music, at least in Uzbekistan.

With Pierre Rousselin, a correspondent for the Paris daily *Le Figaro*, my hitch with Tamar in 1992 was part comic opera, part travelogue and, more dramatically, a story of international intrigue.

Its walls papered with photos of naked women -- all art, Tamar insisted, not creeping perversion, he begged us to understand -- Tamar's garage housed all the comforts of home, which it was. Bed, breakfast and brakes were all the same. Before we hit the road, Tamar thought a visit to his stove, pillow, TV and wrenches was in order. He was, after all, not just your average retired Soviet army veteran. Sixty at the time, and five years into his pension, Tamar strutted in his old but still pressed olive green army uniform that made him look more like a general than the tank mechanic he'd been. Two stars decorated his uniform. Under his official jacket, Tamar wore a shirt and tie. Without the accompanying officer's style large hat and its red band, gold-colored braids, and large star above the visor, his uniform lacked power. Trim and lean, Tamar looked every inch a general, although he could have used six more inches to clinch the deal. A sidearm, a grenade, a megaphone, and a flashing red light that he slapped on the dash as his siren roared on command, warning other drivers of his arrival and quick departure, were all part of his uniformed power. To add to Tamar's mystique, enough antennas sprung from his car to make it appear that he was the defense minister. His pension, Tamar said, allowed him to wear his uniform as long as he lived, a guarantee that others in the neighborhood probably hadn't been warned about.

English wasn't Tamar's first language; Russian wasn't mine either, and neither was Uzbek or Tajik. But Tamar and I knew sign language well, while maps offer another universal language. Besides, names like Tashkent, Samarkand and Leninabad (now Khujand) are easily understood in any language to be foreign, as are their locations. Tamar's understanding of English far exceeded his oral skills. My message was clear as I pointed to a rag on the dash and at Tamar's pet grenade that rolled from beneath the driver's seat. Pierre and I didn't check whether the grenade was live. In a flash, Tamar put two and two together, wrapped the grenade in the rag, and saved us all from possible oblivion.

Tamar drove as if he were heading to defend Stalingrad against the Nazis in World War II. Instead, he was driving Pierre and me along a warped triangle from Tashkent, Uzbekistan's capital, south to the ancient imperial Islamic capital of Samarkand, on to war worried Leninabad in neighboring Tajikistan, and back to Tashkent. As our journey might have been advertised, we swept cross-country without another hitch.

Patience wasn't etched in Tamar's DNA. He held the power

and wanted every driver on the asphalt between Tashkent, Samarkand and Tajikistan to know that truth. No car outraced Tamar's Moskvitch. Siren wailing and red light flashing, we whizzed past all objects, cows or cars. He saved the shouting for other drivers and border guards but said nothing to inert farmers.

"If he thinks he can pass me in his crappy Mercedes, I'll show him," was my interpretation of Tamar's angry language that I didn't fully understand. Tamar gunned his feisty Moskvitch and left the Mercedes to pick cotton near a melon field. Speeding where speeding had no limits wasn't all bad; it meant that we had time to stop and buy apples from a roadside stand to help the local economy as Uzbekistan is fertile country.

Pierre and I were reporting from the new nations of the old Soviet Union and chronicling the flight of Jews to Israel and the United States. This was the global story, serious business that would also force Pierre and me to hitch by air to Moscow, Baku, in Azerbaijan, and Tbilisi in Georgia. Earlier and alone, I had previously done similar reporting from Moscow, Leningrad (now St. Petersburg again) and L'vov, now L'viv, in Ukraine.

With his Hebrew name, his old Soviet army uniform, and his supercharged car, Tamar was the perfect man to help the Jewish Agency find and ferry Jews from Uzbekistan and Tajikistan to Israel. Fearing war and economic hardship in the wake of the Soviet Union's collapse, many Jews wanted out. In his homey garage, Tamar kept a photo of Jerusalem as a reminder of his task and his dormant religious roots. His family history, one of being internal refugees, was another reminder of fear and flight. As a boy, Tamar said, he fled with his family from Minsk in what became Belarus to escape the invading Nazis during World War II. Siberia was the family's first safe landing. That pit stop was far enough away from the war, but Siberia's ice didn't invite refugees to hang out for long. Eventually, Tamar and his family landed in Tashkent, where Pierre and I met him. With his pistol, wrapped grenade, uniform and car, Tamar was in charge of his own destiny, and ours.

Pierre and I were welcomed in the neighborhood because the Jewish Agency wanted the story to reach the world. We wanted, in turn, to learn more about the story and tell it. The story had many hues, however. Israel wanted to retrieve as many Soviet Jews as possible, to save them from possible war and to boost Israel's population while settling many of the new Israelis in the Palestinian West Bank. Adding Israelis to the Jewish settlements or building more settlements in the West Bank squeezed the Palestinians ever more tightly and raised more questions about whether the settlements violated international law.

Tamar, Pierre, and I passed every car in sight between Tashkent and the beautiful remains of old Samarkand. On to Tajikistan, we roared, the danger of a spreading war becoming more real. Nothing slowed us down, not even border crossings, as Tamar's menacing tactics never failed. Tamar's sound and light show did double duty as we skimmed across hills and valleys, visited families and Israeli officials aiding local Jews who wanted to leave their old homes for new ones, and many who weren't sure what to do. We even saw children playing a video baseball game, which astonished me. Danger or great risk never seemed closer than riding with Tamar and his wrapped grenade. Until, that is, air travel was factored in.

Our travel plans became complicated when Pierre and I tried to fly from Tashkent to Baku in Azerbaijan, on the Caspian Sea. That was a thousand miles by air, but no flight existed. Tamar was gone from our lives, but hitching wasn't. Our only realistic option was to fly 1,735 miles west to Moscow, pay $20 to a woman slumped in a seat behind a hazy window just off the tarmac, hang around for days hoping that our plane would come in, and fly 1,200 miles back east to Baku. Pierre and I made that hitch work almost like a jaunt across town.

After a few days of interviews in Baku, we plotted a sprint across the Caucasus Mountains to Tbilisi in the newly independent nation of Georgia. To reach Tbilisi by air from Baku, a man in a World War II era trench coat whispered to us, "You just have to find the pilot and ask how much money he wants." The pilot wanted $25 or 10,000 rubles, for each of us. Pierre and I paid up. A small plane ferried Pierre and me the 280 miles to Tbilisi, then another Wild East town, just in time to check our guns at a hotel. Pierre and I carried no guns, of course, but everyone else in the hotel seemed to because gangs ruled. The gun rack at the hotel entrance was full.

Russian-built Moskova sedan

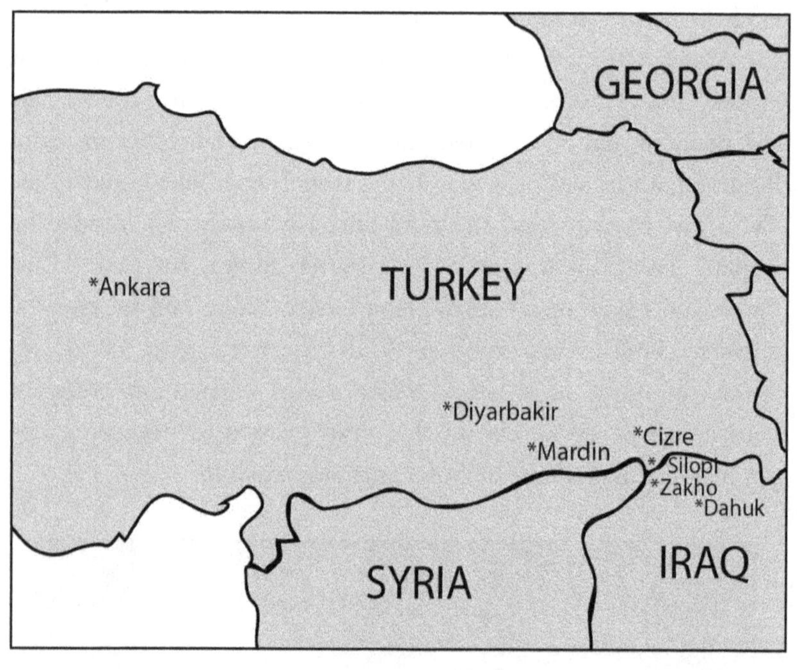
GEORGIA
TURKEY
*Ankara
*Diyarbakir
*Mardin
*Cizre
*Silopi
*Zakho
*Dahuk
SYRIA
IRAQ

8 | RIDING SHOTGUN WITH RAMAZAN AND SALAAM

Amrikee! American! Basin! Journalist! And I had a Turkish press card, useless in Iraq, to prove it. The old Kurdish man urged me and my driver Salaam to the front of the long line of cars waiting to board a shaky pontoon bridge without sides. If there was any doubt that I was home again in Kurdistan, Northern Iraq, the bridge and the welcome removed it all. The Kurds wanted their story told. And I wanted to tell it again, a year after fleeing under the gun with fifteen other journalists and thousands of Kurds from Iraq to Turkey. This time, in March 1992, the war with Saddam Hussein was on low boil. But the Kurds were using the boil time to craft a small autonomous zone that today still breathes in their Iraq. Many would question my decision to return to the Kurdish story after my hazardous entry to Iraqi Kurdistan and subsequent escape to Turkey a year earlier. But my mind allowed only my questions, and answers still to come from the Kurds.

This time Ankara, Turkey's capital, was my launch pad into Iraqi Kurdistan. Ankara thrust me more safely, if not faster, into the story. Turkish Kurds had their own conflict with Turkey's government, a far different brew from that of their brothers and sisters in Iraq with Saddam Hussein. I skirted through Turkey's war against its own Kurds on the long road from Diyarbakir, a large Kurdish city in Turkey, to the Iraqi border near where I had fled across the Khabur River on a raft twelve months earlier.

When Kurds in Turkey or Iraq burped, the official government on either side of the border retaliated, and the Kurds bled.

With help from Kurds in Ankara, my next stop came into view. That was a caravanserai just inside Diyarbakir's old city walls, a long home run from an old Silk Road just outside the walls. The road led south to the town of Mardin, then east along the Turkish-Syrian border to a crossing of the Khabur River south into Iraq, Iraqi Kurdistan.

Ramadan greeted me in Diyarbakir, Turkey's unofficial Kurdish capital. The Muslim month of fasting, prayer, and reflection had no adverse effect on my diet. My health, in fact, improved because I was the only guest at the renovated caravanserai, which for some five hundred years was a rest and rehabilitation dalliance on the trade route east. Hotel workers, all Turkish Kurds, treated me with princely care. If the workers cheated and ate during daytime, they swallowed in the kitchen, not in public.

Most Kurds are Sunni Muslims, believers but not extremists. With no qualms attached, they fed me three squares a day for a long weekend and urged friends to help me find risky and elusive transport to Iraq. They wanted to help me, and I needed their help. That mutual aid pact was ideal for the Kurds and me, and soon would be ready-made for Iraqi Kurdistan.

In a thick notebook I sketched my three-room suite, with its low arches, curved ceilings and sublime eastern atmosphere. Despite my artistic limitations, I drafted the renovated hotel's exotic charm from the outside: two levels of arches, six large ones on the ground floor and six smaller arches above, with all the arches overlooking a large courtyard that embraced gardens, trees and tables for dining. The archway to the pool was opposite the courtyard entrance. The caravanserai looked like a large and inviting motel in a quaint New Mexico town. In the days of camels and horses and trade along silk roads, that's exactly what a caravanserai was: an overnight stop for caravans and their weary travelers. Animals were stabled in the courtyard, shops provided supplies, while traders and travelers slept in quarters like mine, although then not as large or as comfortable.

While waiting to be fed, I plumbed hotel workers for information about the ongoing confrontation between the Turkish government and the Kurdish Workers' Party, the PKK. Wandering comes naturally to me, so I hoofed around town and talked to shopkeepers and their customers, begging for a ride.

After I returned to the caravanserai following my third day in town, things swung in my favor. His name was Ramazan, a driver who said he knew the road to Iraq and was willing to take me all the way. Ramazan was a blank sheet to me. All I knew was that he was a Kurd, which to me at that time and place meant that I could trust him. Ramazan had as much, maybe more, reason to wonder whether he could trust me, an American journalist. That was a gamble he was willing to take because he trusted my willingness to tell the Kurdish story. Without saying so explicitly, we reached a balance of trust and never had a sliver of doubt about whether we could trust each other.

The drive through heavily damaged Kurdish towns took numerous daylight hours. Except for burned out cars, trucks and buildings, our trip lacked other ambient scenery. My Turkish press card, useful in this neighborhood, eased us through army checkpoints, through town after town. All I heard was, "Journalist, American. Okay, you can go." Sometimes soldiers made executive decisions on the spot. At other times, walkie-talkies came into play. In every case, we drove on. One overly zealous but fairly well read soldier insisted that I was Jewish.

"Salome," he said, probably thinking of Shalom, "that's Jewish."

"No," I answered, "it's an Arabic name, like Salaam," although I didn't explain the complex history of my family name. An Arabic name itself is hardly a free pass among Turks or Kurds. Saddam Hussein, a Sunni Arab, made a game of killing Kurds. The soldier didn't believe that Salome was an Arabic name, but his warrior gun remained holstered, and he didn't call for reinforcements. I dropped the dispute, so Ramazan and I could drive peacefully to meet the next platoon and biblical scholar.

In his Renault Toros, a vintage auto with brake fluid and a flywheel that had all its teeth, Ramazan and I wheeled past the town of Mardin and then east along the border with Syria. All the way to the Iraqi border the scenes evoked a distant, sometimes beautiful, past that still echoed in 1992. Four men scattered seeds from bags hung at their waist. Spring planting was the purpose. Equality lay around me, too. To our right rode a man on a donkey. To our left a woman rode her donkey. Kurdish women I had met trained as fighters. A mist-covered valley of rectangular green fields south and below Mardin looked so much like the ocean that Ramazan was forced to insist that it was all farmland. "See the animals," he said in the local dialect. "Yes," I answered in the same dialect.

The center of the Kurdish town of Silopi at the Iraqi border in Turkey resembled the combat zone it had been hours before. Tires still burned in the town of Cizre, a nearby community of Turkish Kurds. Conditions in Silopi and Cizre offered fresh evidence of the deep divide between Turkey's Kurds and Turkey's government.

We picked up a hitchhiker, a Kurd, in Silopi. That could have been me, anywhere. By habit I usually picked up hitchhikers because I've been one so often. Helping a hiker is also another way to learn what's happening in a region and about the people who live there. Ramazan didn't object to our courtesy.

Ramazan and I parted soon after at the Ibrahim Khalil Bridge over the Khabur River. Our drive from Diyarbakir was less than two hundred miles, but the many obstacles along the way made the drive take much longer than it should have. Ramazan would return to Diyarbakir on the same old Silk Road, but without silk.

I headed to Zakho, Iraqi Kurdistan. At that moment, I was the only person allowed to cross the bridge into Iraq. My blue American passport was magical again. Was Saddam Hussein violating the no-fly zone in Iraq that was part of the truce that ended the first Persian Gulf War? I aimed to answer that question. Saddam's fuel and food blockade was punishing the Iraqi Kurds, and I also wanted to learn how much harm the blockade was doing. Intensely divided, the Iraqi Kurds were struggling but slowly succeeding to carve out a zone of their own in their Iraq.

After I strolled across the Khabur River bridge, the best bridge I'd see in all of Iraq, I starting hitching again, scrambling for a lift to nearby Zakho. Lucky once more, I hailed a United Nations police officer from Poland who was willing to play Good Samaritan. He was going my way. His name, the officer said, began with a "J" and ended with an "I". That's the way I heard his name, and I didn't ask the man to spell it. Too many vowels and consonants flowed between the "J" and the "I" to count. In my notebook, I mangled his name this way, "J…….i."

Within an hour of reaching Zakho, I stumbled on Salaam Khalid. The gods were with me, I thought. Then I stumbled again and hitched my immediate future to Salaam's. That was a mistake, a minor one in my world of mistakes, but another in a series of lifelong learning experiences on the verge. Instinctively, we trusted each other. Salaam and I encountered no blinking yellow lights in Iraqi Kurdistan, and if he spotted such a rare bird, he ignored it along with lights of all colors. Salaam, no relation to me, said he'd suffered from a painful toothache for four long years. Hard to imagine such long suffering for a toothache, but who was I to doubt Salaam? Perhaps the worsening ache explained his anger, although many other environmental factors could explain his angst. Salaam drove like one angry Kurd. He roared through towns, threatening to run over crippled tribesmen, women and children, barely pulling up short, as if to warn the heedless that the next time he wouldn't stop. Salaam careered along narrow, muddy mountain tracks as if no crater were large enough to hold us. Then Salaam decided he'd had enough.

Only after he found a friend, a local dentist, did Salaam's attitude improve. Fifteen minutes after he ascended to the second floor of a building in the city of Erbil, Salaam emerged happy, and one aching tooth lighter. The dentist took the old-fashioned string and yank route.

"It's free, ten dinars (about $1), and I get relaxed," Salaam said, smiling as he hadn't smiled in many moons, his life on the upswing. Everyone, including me, in Iraqi Kurdistan was safer because Salaam Khalid could smile again. How long Salaam's eyes would sparkle was another matter. To stanch the blood from the space where his tooth had been, Salaam stuffed a filthy rag. Within two hours, he found a corner table where he could slurp potato soup, gum a little bread, and chug two made-in-America soft drinks. Then Salaam stuffed the rag back into his mouth.

Fate bound Salaam and me together, or so it seemed. A double hitch and a boost from fate lay ahead. Purely by accident, I met one professor, one lecturer, and two women doctoral students from the University of London's School of Oriental and African Studies. The students and their profs were headed to the land of the Yazidis, themselves professors of an ancient eclectic religion that is pre-Roman and pre-just-about-every-other religion in that ancient land. At first the visitors from England resisted my overtures to join them. But I begged, cajoled, and promised to behave if they let me tag alone. I took a vow of silence, promised to ask no questions of the Yazidis, and not to interfere in any way with the academy's mission. After we struck a deal in the Kurdish city of Dahuk just south of Zakho, I was allowed to follow my new friends into a past so deep as to seem impenetrable, incomprehensible. Only later did the sunrise reveal how far into antiquity I had hitched from a simple beginning.

For two years, hitching drove me from a small town in Massachusetts twenty-five miles away to a Jesuit college where I studied philosophy, religion, French, logic, rhetoric, English and American literature, and history. (I prefer to forget the math and science.) For nearly five years, I was based in Jerusalem, home to the three major Abrahamic faiths. Two years into my stint as a journalist in the cradle of three major Western religions, I witnessed a band of Samaritans, an offshoot of Judaism, celebrate their 3636th Passover on Mount Gerizim, their holiest site, near the Palestinian West Bank city of Nablus. A few years after that, I wandered into the Syrian town of Ma'alula, where locals still speak ancient Aramaic, the vernacular in the region 2,000 years earlier. Without a hint of prescience, I figured Hinduism, Buddhism, and other isms awaited me, the hitching son of a variant of New England Puritanism whose ancestral roots lay in Syria.

Passing through time with the Samaritans and Yazidis was like shuffling through life staring at Barney the Blacksmith shoeing horses in the 1950s on the way to my next lives. The difference and time, of course, were of centuries versus decades.

The Yazidis taught me much about themselves, other Kurds, Saddam Hussein's Iraq, and humanity. My new Yazidi friends were Kurds who shared a common Indo-European language with other Kurds. But Yazidis, unlike most other Kurds, aren't Muslims. Scoffed at even by other Kurds for their religious diversion, Yazidis are at the bottom of Iraq's ethnic and religious totem pole because they are neither Arabs nor Muslims. A minority within a minority, the Yazidis are refugees in their own land. When an opportunity arose, which was almost daily, Yazidis were hunted and killed, usually by Saddam Hussein's Sunni Arab military and minority government. Kurds in general were the targets of Saddam's wrath, notably in the late 1980s, when he unleashed Al Anfal against Iraq's Kurds. Al Anfal means, literally, the spoils or booty of war, vengeance, to get even with an enemy in previous conflicts. An estimated 50,000 to 100,000 Iraqi Kurds were rounded up and murdered in 1988. Their sin was siding with Iran during a border conflict in the 1970s, a war that left Iraq's Kurds naked after the governments of Iraq and Iran made peace, and the United States agreed to the truce and abandoned the Kurds.

Conditions worsened drastically for the Yazidis after the Iraqi branch of Al Qaida, followed by the even more wildly extremist Islamic State of Iraq and Syria (ISIS), swept through the region in the second decade of the twenty-first century. ISIS fighters were hunting for Yazidis, who were viewed as double heretics because they weren't Arabs or Muslims, and ISIS found them in their mountain villages and religious sanctuaries. Numerous reports filtered from the Yazidi's Sinjar region of Iraq about villages being destroyed, believers being murdered, and Yazidi women being taken as sex slaves. Several thousand Yazidis were trapped in villages before Kurdish fighters, known as peshmergas, (those who face death) rescued them. Because of the help the Yazidis received from the peshmergas, many Yazidi men joined forces with those Kurdish fighters, their ethnic brothers and sisters.

Two years after I had watched the West Bank Samaritans conduct their religious rituals, Salaam and I hitched our wagon to the academy's and headed to the mountain home of the Yazidi people. Through a cold, lashing rain that resembled a Caribbean hurricane without the wind and warmth, I reached the Yazidi village of Ribebi, southeast of Dahuk. The date was April 1, 1992, April Fool's Day. And that's no joke. The London visitors were expected and were greeted like prophets of a sort. I was ignored, which suited my role perfectly. The women in the village were especially welcoming of the women students. Their embraces weren't shocking because Yazidi religious tenets are passed on through their women.

A Kurd and a Sunni Muslim, definitely not a Yazidi, Salaam caught my drift and followed my lead. Though he had never met a Yazidi, Salaam kept quiet as he gazed in awe at our surroundings. Like many of the drivers I met on the road, Salaam had an intuitive knack for knowing where to go, what to say and do, and why.

A breakfast feast was offered, almost more than the Yazidis possessed. Hungry and refusing to reject the offering and violate local courtesies, I ate. Boiled eggs, tea, cheese, bread and olives graced the table. Others did the talking. Keeping my vow, I listened and observed. Several religious leaders spoke and explained the principles of Yazidi beliefs, about which the London visitors elaborated.

The Yazidis have been around for centuries too numerous to count. They would hang on, but they've paid the price. From being one of the first believers, maybe the very first, to go the one God route, they fell behind other believers of other faiths who badly outnumbered them. Although they adopted many of the beliefs of the newcomers surrounding them, the Yazidis never shed the label of "the other." Outcasts might as well have been their new name because they were so different. Others rejected them or tried to exterminate them. For other Kurds and local Arabs, rejecting the Yazidis was a way of raising their own flag atop the mountain. By rejecting the Yazidis and their history and status in the land, their neighbors hoped to disown that part of their own histories, cultures and space.

That old human story is without borders. It's a way for each ascending group to rewrite its own history by rejecting a past they deem to reflect poorly on themselves. The more a people whitewash or erase their past, the more they can reject what they wish and cleanse their own record. That happens everywhere. It's happening in the United States today, united being an outdated word for these times, and history being what Americans don't want to know.

All the Yazidis wanted was to be left alone in their own space. They weren't usurping power or threatening anyone. But they were different, which makes all the difference.

One of the doctoral students planned to live with the Yazidis for a year. The other student intended to stay only a month.

When the time came for me and Salaam to slink from their village the Yazidis offered me the opportunity to visit their most sacred site, a cave called Lalish. I begged off, foolishly, because I had an appointment to see a foreign commander about war, a story as old as the Yazidis and humanity.

OO

War is combat between truths and lies to support political as much as military objectives. In Iraqi Kurdistan, truths were hidden to protect the guilty. For example, U. S. military reports from commanders on the ground about Turkish air raids against Kurds in Iraq were scrubbed at higher levels to avoid upsetting NATO ally Turkey, where a vital NATO air base is located.

Turkish jets were bombing Kurdish enclaves in Iraq because Turkish Kurds, the Kurdish Workers Party, were hiding there. So claimed the Turkish government. But Salaam and I found no Turkish Kurds hiding in Iraq at the time, and neither did the U.S. led coalition. Neither did I uncover evidence that Saddam Hussein's helicopters were attacking Iraqi Kurds from the air and thus violating the truce that ended the first Persian Gulf War. What I did see, first hand, was Saddam's fuel and food embargo work its cruel and constant damage against Iraq's Kurdish minority. Saddam's forces allowed the Iraqi Kurds to travel into Arab zones to purchase much-needed gasoline. As the Kurds attempted to return to their own areas, Saddam's soldiers seized the gasoline from the Kurds and poured it on the ground. The Kurds lost twice in that transaction: They paid Saddam's Arabs for the gasoline, but they were never able to use it.

Two days before Salaam and I met the academy and the Yazidis, we slithered in the mud up to the Qandil Bridge farther south in Iraq. Navigating the muddy trail by itself was a gamble. I peered out the car window and saw no dirt, no road. Only open space and the valley below came into view because we were riding along the pebble thin edge of the road above an abyss. On sleepless nights, I still see rocks from the edge of the road dive to the abyss below, but Salaam held steady. Trust in Salaam, I thought, because by then I had no choice.

As we approached the long line of cars leading to the Qandil, I thought of Yogi Berra, the great New York Yankees baseball philosopher whose thoughts carried deeper meanings than his naked words. "When you come to a fork in the road," Yogi said long ago, "take it." At the Qandil Bridge, my Yogi thought was, when you get to a raft, a leaky boat, or a pontoon barge in Iraqi Kurdistan, take it because that's the closest you'll get to a real bridge.

The Qandil Bridge was actually a pontoon raft or barge; twenty-five other vehicles were lined up waiting their turn to shoot the bridge and the river ahead. The pontoons were made of metal. Wood planks, fourteen feet wide and thirty feet long, covered the pontoons, creating a craft that was supposed to float. Two-by-fours rimmed the raft to give the appearance that cars couldn't roll overboard. When Salaam and I crossed, the raft carried Salaam's car, three small trucks, and forty other humans. Salaam and I crossed quickly because we went to the head of the line, and no one complained.

"Amrikee," shouted Salaam. The word was magical again, and the small human sea parted.

Figuring I had a better chance to survive if the raft listed and the cargo rolled off, I stood outside the car, holding on. Salaam stayed in the driver's seat, ready to drive into the water and gun the car before the drowning arrived with the flood. Well, I thought, it's Salaam's car. On a cold, windy afternoon, we barged across the hundred yards of fast flowing water in roughly three minutes. On the opposite shore, a cable attached to the barge and pulled by a tractor yanked us across. As part of this high wire act, two other cables were hooked to the barge to keep it more or less straight as the tractor and the main cable jerked the barge to land-ho. The drama continued when recruits on the far shore aligned ramps with the raft so Salaam could drive his car from the raft to land without going through a car wash. Remarkably, Salaam and I, along with everyone else on board, survived the crossing. How lucky I was, I thought, to have had the experience of standing under a bridge in a blizzard on Route 146 in Worcester, Massachusetts, bumming a ride home from college, and cursing motorists who ignored me.

One of my many wild surprises on the roadside rang out in the wilderness at the Khabur Bridge, as I was about to head back to Diyarbakir in Turkey. By the road near the bridge stood a lonely telephone booth, literally in the middle of nothing. I had filed stories from that bare telephone box and had just finished filing another. Miraculously, my stories reached the Cox Newspapers Washington Bureau when I wasn't certain they would cross the bridge. A Tandy 200 computer did the trick. The Tandy had rubber cups that I used to cover each end of the phone. Then I squeezed the cups tightly to make sure no precious, mysterious signals escaped, pressed a few computer keys, and hoped the magic would work. Each time it worked, probably with a few glitches. After I finished filing my last story, just before I headed across the bridge to thumb a ride back to Diyarbakir, I heard a familiar voice and saw a familiar face. It was an Associated Press reporter I knew well.

"You're the reason I'm here," the visiting scribe shouted, his voice ringing with mocked anger. "Your stories, that's why I'm here." That was an unusual way to learn that the stories I was writing had reached the outside world and were having an effect. Later I learned that those same stories were published in a London newspaper as well as in Cox newspapers.

In that way, I left Iraq, again. My departure was calm, without further surprise. Kurdish towns along the road to Diyarbakir were still occupied by smoldering tires and Turkish soldiers in a long and bitter war that received little attention outside of Turkish Kurdistan. A decade later, however, my exit from Kabul, Afghanistan's capital, and the subsequent drive to Islamabad, Pakistan's capital, was a top of the line hitchhiker's escape.

A mere $1,000 paid for my treacherous seven-hour drive from Kabul to the border crossing at Torkham, Pakistan. That journey was a bit steep in silver but safe because three Afghans I had worked with and knew well were at the wheel. We paid our respects to the four journalists who were murdered along that trail, ridiculously called Highway 7, during the American invasion of Afghanistan a few months earlier. Despite the tease, I never came close to bedding down with those four courageous journalists who are now permanently missing. Real hitching came at the border, on the Pakistani side. Alone in a mini-van built to carry thirteen, my safety was assured. One driver, three different gunmen, less than four hours and 150 miles later, I was in Islamabad. I felt like a prisoner in that van as we zoomed on the wrong side of the asphalt through the twisting Khyber Pass and the city of Peshawar, so fast that no one outside the van could figure out who I was or what I was doing, which was the point.

Not long after I hit Islamabad, I fell so violently ill that I left my hotel room sprawled on a baggage cart. Without hotel and airline help, I never would have been able to board the plane bound for the United Arab Emirates. Without hospice care from Bulgarian flight attendants in the rear of the plane, I wouldn't have been able to sprawl, shivering, under all the blankets available, on a section with three seats near the toilets. Without assistance, enough sustaining water and orange juice would have been beyond my reach. On to London another jet roared, then yet another from Heathrow to Washington.

A typical caravanserai in Diyarbakir
Photo Credit: Wikimedia — Dosseman

BASIN KARTI ■ Press Card

T.C.
BAŞBAKANLIK
BASIN YAYIN
VE ENFORMASYON
GENEL MUDURLUĞU

REPUBLIC OF TURKEY
PRIME MINISTRY
GENERAL DIRECTORATE
OF PRESS AND
INFORMATION

ADI-SOYADI
Full Name LOUIS J.SALOME

GOREVI
Occupation COX NEWSPAPERS
MUHABİR-

EV ADRESI
Home address BEST OTEL
ANKARA

№ 01722

Kurdish Leader Masoud Barzani

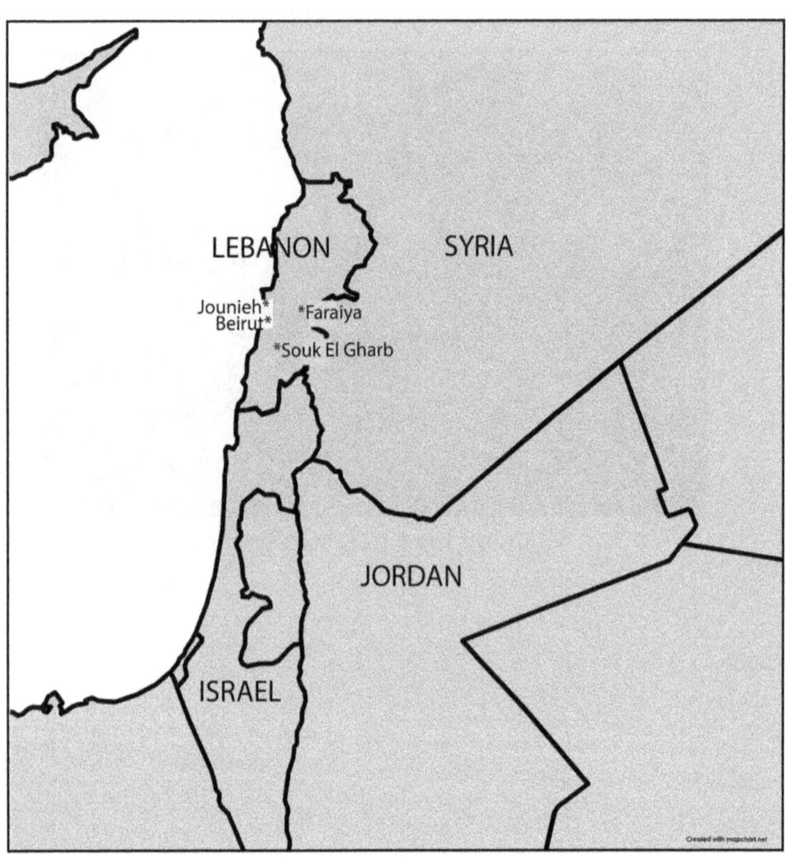
LEBANON
SYRIA
Jounieh*
Beirut*
*Faraiya
*Souk El Gharb
JORDAN
ISRAEL
Created with mapchart.net

9 | SAILING TO LEBANON

Khalil wheeled into the lot at Faraiya. A brilliant sun splattered across the resort and its tanning guests. Angled all about Khalil's powder blue Mercedes were BMWs, Range Rovers, more Mercedes, even a Jaguar, and other low-priced wagons of varying colors. A Ferrari, however, was nowhere in sight. A chic ski and summer resort less than an hour's drive into the mountains east-northeast of battered Beirut, Faraiya was home to mid-level wealth escaping from Lebanon's long civil war, if only on weekends. The really rich fled the country. The poor stayed behind to fight for one cause or another or to hide because they lacked the means to leave or a welcome mat elsewhere.

Khalil and his Mercedes were my hitch into this small slice of the war, and to many other pieces of Lebanon's conflict, from crumbling urban basement hideouts all the way to the front at the once beautiful but now leveled mountain town of Souk el-Gharb (Western Market). In Faraiya, Khalil and I watched bathing beauties sunning by the pool, urging us to understand their plight:

"What do you want us to do, die?" one gorgeous woman asked, rhetorically. As the sun rained down on the sunbathers, Khalil and I ate fine meals and heard tales of how beautiful the resort is during all seasons, especially during the season of peace when garbage was collected and dumped elsewhere, which during my visit was some fifteen years earlier and two years distant. Of the many chalets with rooms to rent in this third week of August in 1989, there were no vacancies.

Capable of get-away speeds, running over rough terrain and zooming to the right or left past traffic a Mercedes was widely used as a tank of war, sometimes even by men shouldering rifles. This was especially true in zones where ports offered easy access from points west, as did Beirut and its sister docks in Lebanon. When Soviet-style communism collapsed in the early nineties, Europe's borders opened, and big cars, bought or stolen, fit for warrior conditions or just expensive and desirable, flowed east by land as well as by sea. Where the big cars didn't reach, older, smaller cars made in Russia, Eastern and Western Europe, and Japan still had useful homes in lots named Bosnia, Croatia, Serbia and Albania. Cars like the wired together 1948 De Soto were useless in war and most other domains.

After we met by chance in the port of Jounieh, north of Beirut, Khalil helped me draw a map of Lebanon in my notebook. We interviewed soldiers, religious and political figures, and civilians around the country. Along the way a mad mosaic of a map came into view, helping me to understand whose guns were where and why. Because Lebanon's a small country, it had almost too many tents and flags for the landscape. Scattered and yet solidified were militias related to various factions: from Christian; to Shiite and Sunni Muslims; to the Druze people, who are Arabs but only off-beat Muslims; to Palestinians in their refugee camps. Even a United Nations peacekeeping force ironically held firm in its own zone in the southwest. Iranian forces, there but hard to identify, filtered in with Lebanese Shiite fighters and Syrian soldiers. Then there was Israel's military linked to its discrete Christian allies in the far south. Hovering over most of the country, and infiltrating where they didn't hover, were Syrian forces. Many Lebanese, notably Christian factions, considered the Syrians as occupiers. I made room on our evolving map for a handful of people – including three generations tucked underground but surviving in the mountain town of Souk el-Gharb at the front itself. Because Khalil and I were in a resort, I was compelled to sneak into a corner of my map the word Faraiya. There I gawked in disbelief as the semi-wealthy enjoyed a little R and R. Khalil, accustomed to the scene, only shrugged.

The war in Lebanon began as a civil conflict with sweeping political, ethnic/religious, and military dimensions. Soon it turned into a proxy war in which the major players used lesser lights to squeeze triggers for them. Conflict evolution dictated that masters and their proxies attract regional players. Even the old *U.S.S. New Jersey* lobbed errant shells into the mountains east of Beirut in the early Eighties, but Ronald Reagan's disastrous stage of the war was finished by the time I reached the old Phoenician shores. Two decades after my first reporting hitch, this Lebanese style war struck harder and wider in Syria. It's difficult to show a direct causal link between the two wars, but the patterns are similar: internal conflicts morphed into proxies that morphed into regional escapades and finally into wars of a broader scale of nationalities and ideologies. Wars, it's been widely and correctly said, are easy to start and brutally difficult to end. They usually exhaust themselves before few can recall why they started and exploded. Syria simmers as it awaits exhaustion.

A flight from Athens to Cyprus had launched me eventually to Jounieh, the Lebanese port where I hooked up with Khalil. A swift Norwegian catamaran, a first for me, filled the time and space from the Cypriot port of Larnaca to Jounieh. Along the way, I interviewed Lebanese who had fled their country but were returning from Paris. "Vagabonds" is how they described themselves. Some were so embarrassed by neighbor killing neighbor that they refused to call themselves Arabs. Reaching back a couple of thousand years, they preferred the name Phoenicians.

It wasn't long before I boarded the *Santa Maria* in Larnaca, Cyprus, with 124 other passengers. Only 120 miles straight on separated Jounieh from Cyprus, but the trip was 127 miles long because the *Santa Maria* had to feint and dodge Syrian and French warships before bobbing and weaving to avoid Syrian shells off Jounieh itself. With only eight passengers, the *Santa Maria* had reached Cyprus two hours behind schedule. The ship was late to pick us up because of heavy shelling at Jounieh. Only eight passengers had boarded in Jounieh before the ship was forced to flee, and a swift catamaran can flee. Most passengers aiming for safety in Cyprus never boarded the ship. Instead they hunkered down for the night behind concrete and sand bags. The *Santa Maria* loitered off shore as long as it could, hoping the noise would stop so it could return to retrieve more passengers in Jounieh. When the artillery continued the captain made a U-turn from the shelling zone to meet me in Cyprus.

Boarding the *Santa Maria* in Larnaca was easy. There was no shelling, no fear. When George said, "We wish to inform our passengers that the American poker table is open in the VIP section," I felt right at home. George operated the *Santa Maria's* concession. On this trip, George filled in for his brother. George's brother normally ran the poker game, took the cut for the house and filled in at the table when needed. But George's brother was stuck in Jounieh, left behind because of the shelling. The American poker table on the *Santa Maria* reminded me of poker games that my grandfather Big Louie, a Syrian immigrant, ran in Millville when I was a kid. But that's another story.

My hitch on the *Santa Maria* was short but even more stimulating than when Dickie McCrohan stopped to help two passionate hounds as we drove to Uxbridge on my way to college. We pulled out of Larnaca under a full moon, beautiful to behold, but hardly ideal for sailing into shellfire. Fifteen minutes from Jounieh, the captain ordered all the lights turned off.

"No smoking," he said, "no lighting matches, and turn off all radios, please." The American poker table went dark. This was no joke. The wheelhouse itself was in darkness, except for lights on the instrument panel. Cleared for docking because the enemy was napping, we zipped into port and dashed off the ship with military precision. As quickly as we left the ship, other passengers – those who missed the earlier passage – boarded, and the *Santa Maria* turned tail back to Cyprus. Safe at home, we heard later. The next day I rode with Khalil in his powder blue Mercedes to see how some Lebanese relaxed by the pool at a mountain resort while most Lebanese suffered and died.

A typical taxi and driver in the Middle East.
Photo: Martin Nangle

Norwegian Catamaran
Photo: Sergey Ashmarin, Creative Commons

*Belgrade
SERBIA
BULGARIA
KOSOVO
*Skopje
MACEDONIA
GREECE
Athens
*

10 | TRAINS, BARGES, AND SMUGGLERS

My experience with train travel began in Woonsocket, a booming urb southeast of Millville in northern Rhode Island. My grandparents discovered its mills, tenements, shops, and grand department store, more than mere miles from their homeland of Greater Syria in the Ottoman Empire. For my mother's parents, the year was 1905. My father's parents, though much younger, arrived in 1908. The city's population was a touch over 28,000 in 1900. By 1910, Woonsocket's population had swelled to more than 38,000. In that ten-year span, my grandparents and their many cousins were among the ten thousand people who came searching for jobs and a better everything. By 1940, the year before I was born, the city's population had climbed to 49,303, less than a thousand short of its peak in 1950. The new immigrants succeeded in their search.

Woonsocket even had a spiffy hotel downtown, near McCarthy's Department Store. An institution on Main Street, McCarthy's was a six-floor gem, with an elevator in which a human operator stood next to or sat on a metal stool and took shoppers to men's shoes, overcoats, ladies' dresses or lingerie. Now that was exciting. The Hotel Blackstone had fifty rooms, a ballroom where sailors from Newport, Rhode Island's navy base came to hoof it on weekends, and a bowling alley in the basement. Don't scoff at the bowling alley, because bowling was and remains a huge sport and social activity in Rhode Island.

Founded in 1889, McCarthy's left Main Street in 1967, and moved to a shopping center. It succumbed in the shopping center in 1989, just after it turned one hundred. Main Street had already died. Woonsocket had gradually fallen back, its jobs evaporating and heading south, its various shops on once-vibrant Main Street closing or moving elsewhere to die.

Hailing the rich French-Canadian immigrant tradition of many of its residents, Woonsocket even swung for the fences in the mid-fifties when it launched a Mardi Gras parade. That was a bold and brilliant idea, but the time and place were slightly off. A full-blown parade in February in New England was too easily blown away by season and snow. Woonsocket's annual Mardi Gras parade and five days of festivities marched from 1954 until 1959, when February betrayed its reach for glory and Woonsocket bowed to New Orleans and its Creole and Cajun history. With a ball but no parade, the tradition has been revived in Woonsocket. Without a parade, however, revelry doesn't float in quite the same way.

Within sight of McCarthy's and the Hotel Blackstone stood a train depot, as perfect a rendition of the genre, and in my mind in as perfect a small city as existed east of the Mississippi. As useful as ever, although not for train service, the depot remains, but passenger trains stopped tooting their arrivals and departures in downtown Woonsocket some sixty-six years ago. The last passenger train left Woonsocket for Providence, Rhode Island's capital, on December 29, 1957, two years before the curtain fell on Woonsocket's Mardi Gras parade. That last train from Woonsocket carried only three passengers, the same number as the ghost train that carried me from the Greek-Macedonian border to Athens thirty-eight years later. In 1929, twenty passenger trains left Woonsocket each day. Maybe I wasn't paying close attention, but I don't recall ever seeing a passenger train chug into town during my twenty-one years of living in the neighborhood. After I moved to Boston for graduate school in 1962, I took the train from nearby Franklin, Massachusetts, to the Massachusetts Bay Colony and back several times. In Boston I took the subway regularly to classes at Boston College and years later rode north and south on Amtrak and the Auto Train a few times. Those trips were my only exposure to regular train travel. Until, that is, I rode with Lawrence of Arabia from Damascus, Syria, to Amman, Jordan; from Moscow to Leningrad (now St. Petersburg again) as the Soviet Union lay dying; on a smugglers' train from Sofia, Bulgaria to Belgrade, Serbia, on that ghost train from Skopje, Macedonia to Athens, and to and from too many other cities to count.

Timing is everything in life, it's often said. If my grandparents had reached Woonsocket during the depths of the city's long slump, they would have caught the first bus to anywhere else. Instead, it was I who pulled out of Woonsocket some sixty years after my grandparents wandered in. First, I found race riots and the KKK in Miami, and national political conventions in Miami Beach. Before, that is, I discovered grand hotels in Europe's and Asia's fabulous cities, and a cave in Somalia, scorpions stalking me when the lights died in Afghanistan, and a twenty-four-hour-train ride through Russia's great northern forests.

OO

Barges floated off the Blackstone River Canal after the railroad chugged into the valley. The iron horse was a decade away from whistling past its prime when I, age six and a half, drifted into Millville, Massachusetts from nearby Woonsocket. That was in the fall of 1947, when I left Miss Oliver at Woonsocket's Vose Street School to join Miss Kennedy's second grade class at Longfellow Elementary in Millville. Working rivers, canals, barges and narrow gauge railways came into view years later in places far from the Blackstone River Valley. My wife Pat and our children, Margaret, then age 5; Mary, then 2, and Andrew, barely age 1, beat me to the tarmac in 1970, when they flew to Miami where I was eyeing a house after riding my internal combustion engine down the East Coast. From then on, I held the family's flight record, which no one envied. Chickens rode with me on a flight from Tashkent, Uzbekistan, west to Moscow. No cackling allowed. To board a flight from Moscow all the way back east to Baku, Azerbaijan, I handed a mysterious woman twenty dollars hard American cash. I asked no questions, and neither did the sad-looking woman who sat slumped, palms up, behind glass at the tarmac's edge. Legal or otherwise, that transaction worked.

After a few days in Baku, I flew west over the Caucasus Mountains to Tblisi, Georgia, a short flight that cost twenty-five dollars. When planes and trains tired of taking me into and out of trouble, nameless floating objects filled the gap. Aging helicopters short on replacement parts rose to the occasion when roads were too clogged with tens of thousands of walking mourners to allow autos to rush to the burial of Iran's revolutionary religious leader.

"Death to America, Death to America."

Louder and louder those shouts rose from the swelling crowd that surrounded me and a mass of reporters gathered in Tehran to observe a nation called to mourn, or else. On the spot, I was forced to hitch again, but I wasn't alone. The moment was early June 1989; the place was Iran's capital: the occasion was the funeral of the Grand Ayatollah Sayyid Ruhollah Mousavi

Khomeini, age 89. For ten years, the man known simply as the Ayatollah or the Ayatollah Khomeini had led Iran's ultra-religious Islamic government. The Ayatollah's revolutionary cohort had replaced the Shah of Iran's autocratic American-backed government – extremist in its own way – that had ruled Iran without restraint for two and a half decades.

The death threats were generic: nothing personal. Generically, they were aimed at the two tall, fair-haired Norwegian journalists flanking me. I could pass for anyone in the region. Still, none of us was thrilled to hear the threats. All we wanted was to hop aboard one of the old American-made helicopters assigned to take all the journalists to the Ayatollah's burial compound in south Teheran. There I would witness the leader's remains fall from the litter that held them, creating even more bedlam than before we had boarded the helicopters. After having slowly escaped the breaths of the shouting crowd on their way to witness Khomeini's burial, I snatched, barely, the last seat on one helicopter. With half of my rump sitting on a seat, and the other half grasping air, I clutched a grip inside the chopper and held on tightly until we reached the burial site. The return trip carried its own drama, but that time I managed to sit wholly inside another helicopter.

OO

William Jefferson Clinton pointed me to a raft on the Sava River in northern Bosnia. Bill Clinton's guidance was real, though his role in that rafting hitch was indirect. Clinton, whom I always felt would have made a great UN secretary general, commissioner of Major League baseball, or king of an African country, was taking a victory lap through London, Belfast and

Dublin, on his way to an American air base in Germany.

Welcomed in London because the United States and the British cherished the Anglo-American special relationship, Clinton had also named former U.S. Senator George Mitchell to broker peace in Northern Ireland. Because he had earned his chops on Northern Ireland, Clinton was embraced as a long lost son and conquering hero in Belfast and Dublin. When he flew to the Ramstein air base in Germany, I tagged along on the White House press plane. That wasn't exactly bumming a ride. The German leg of Clinton's journey was heavy with international ballast. He went to cheer on and send off American soldiers headed to Bosnia to help enforce the Bosnian Peace Treaty/Dayton Peace Accords that would stanch the five-year Bosnian wars. My assignment was to reach the American base at Tuzla, Bosnia, on or before the peace deal was to be signed in Paris on December 14, 1995.

Alone after Clinton and the soldiers paid perfunctory tribute to each side of their mission, I bummed a ride with a car full of soldiers to Heidelberg, Germany. From Heidelberg, where I stocked up on cold weather gear, sipped holiday grog, and watched elderly Germans dance, the road ahead looked easy. Flying to Budapest, Hungary, was simple enough. There the trail grew tricky. I was to trace the trail the soldiers would take in order to determine whether proper preparations had been made to ease their way. Through Hungary and later into Croatia, I found roads, bridges, and air bases far behind the timetables scheduled to accommodate the arriving American boots. I would reach Tuzla before the ink settled on the peace treaty and well ahead of almost every American and NATO soldier.

From Budapest I flew to Zagreb, Croatia's capital. Armed with a healthy breakfast, the next day I rented a car, hired a translator, and drove two and a half hours southeast to the Sava River on the Croatian-Bosnian border. Two bridges, one exclusively for railroad traffic, across the river were destroyed during the war. A planned pontoon bridge for the expected military traffic was still on a drawing board somewhere. And I can't swim. Fortunately or otherwise, a raft was anchored on the Croatian side of the Sava. The Croatian raft was so underpowered that a tugboat and steel cables were required to jerk the raft across the river to Bosnia. It's difficult to imagine such a contraption during peacetime, but anything goes in a war. When the time came to cross the Sava from Bosnia back to Croatia, the raft pulled by a tugboat was no longer seaworthy, or even river worthy. My choice was to stay in Bosnia and leave my rental car in Croatia or find another hitch back across the Sava to Croatia. Out of the mist my new hitch appeared; a small boat without sides and with an engine so wispy its putt-putt whisper could barely be heard. So I held steady and hitched again, back to Croatia. To reach the American base in Tuzla, Bosnia, the end of a journey that began in London, I drifted from the city of Split in Croatia through the aftermath of a great blizzard. Don't go, I was warned; there's fighting along the way; the mountain road is blocked, and it's too dangerous. Sure enough, the snow was neck high and the road was more of a danger than the fighting, which was an exaggerated threat. I slid into Tuzla well ahead of the main force of American troops who arrived just in time for Christmas dinner.

OO

My blue American passport stood out in the sea of red. The Jordanian officer didn't have to announce me as "The American.

Where's the American?" In Arabic or in English no interpretation was necessary. To the unaware, it might have seemed like I was being nabbed. But the atmosphere told a different story. As he spoke, the officer waved my American passport, a little blue booklet that carried more weight than its appearance suggested. Last on the list to be called, I stood out further when I smiled and strolled forward in the rocking and rickety railroad car to accept the papers that hailed my legitimacy. The officer had held all the passports since we crossed the Syrian border into Jordan. Nothing more was said after my passport found its home. We were in the Jordanian desert city of Al-Mafraq, eighty-six miles from Damascus, Syria, my starting point, and fifty-one miles from Amman, Jordan, my destination.

Traveling slowly through time as well as space, I was creeping along on the Hejaz Railway. Nothing about that train was new in early 1990, when I hopped aboard to taste its rich history and stale present. New for the railway was in 1908, when its first engine roared from Istanbul to Damascus to Medina in the Hejaz region of Arabia, hence the name Hejaz Railway. Like the long-dead Ottoman Empire itself, the intervening years were a sad model of decay. My purpose was to inhale the past and the railway's earliest passengers, all the Turks, Arabs and other believers who wished to reach their sacred city of Mecca. The railway's last spike was pounded into the sand in Medina, Islam's second-holiest site. No Muslim pilgrim ever stepped off the Hejaz train in Mecca. When I rode the narrow gauge antique the vessel had only enough track to enter Amman, Jordan.

The fleeting past, and a little adventure, nestled in my mind when I boarded at the colonial era station in Damascus. All I wanted was to sniff history, to feel the rough hide of its unending connection to the present, and to ponder the creased lines of its changeless faces. All I knew was that desert dunes lay ahead, along with a few camels and Bedouin camps. Convenience and speed I never expected, and never received, though I was treated more as a guest than as a British or French colonizer. This was a journey of a different kind. Passengers didn't need me, and I didn't need them, so all bargaining chips were off the table. Almost fifty other passengers carried no urgency to tell their stories, and I wasn't pleading to listen and write about them. I ended up telling the story anyway, almost incidentally.

My journey took nine hours and forty-five minutes to zoom 137 miles. A hurried traveler could make the same trip by car in three hours, or fly in forty minutes. My first-class ticket cost a princely $4.25, one-way, but I never learned the meaning of first class. A second-class ticket was $2.50. All the comfort anyone could inhale was free, as were the facilities, straight into the desert off the caboose. The track was narrow gauge, which meant the train could outpace a camel caravan without derailing. The passenger cars were made of wood. When the train jerked to a stop, the doors swung open and the windows, never fixed in place, slipped north or south. Holes in the floor allowed passengers to see the tracks and count the sand pebbles as the rolling stock rumbled to Amman.

Eight decades after its inaugural run, the Hejaz train was running out of time. Badly out of date, the cars trembled as they rolled, slowly. But the train was still useful. The train to and from Woonsocket had stalled thirty-two years before. Though much newer and in far better condition than its Hejaz cousin, the Woonsocket version was useless to local residents because, thirty years before, it had stopped serving the people of

Woonsocket, the bottom line dictating where and when it ran and whom it served.

Riding the rails to Amman I learned as much about the present as the past. Something like the Hejaz Railway exists everywhere. The train was no longer slick, efficient or even convenient. But it was cheap, which masked its inconvenience. People put up with such broken antiquities because they have no choice or feel helpless against forces beyond their control. Although well outside the circle of helplessness, I chose to board that Lawrence of Arabia-era train to ride with history long after the train sparked wonder in all who rode it or watched it in awe. From all appearances, the other passengers with me had no choice. This was a story as old as people and cultures: the poorer the place, the poorer the people. Inconveniences aren't seen as such because alternatives don't exist.

Though they lacked stories to share and pleas for help, a few passengers were eager to please me, a visitor. In Dera'a, the last stop in Syria, and the town where the savage war in Syria was to begin two decades later, a man bought me a bottle of water and an egg sandwich after a heavy overnight rain and deep mud had thwarted my attempt to help the local economy. An elderly Lebanese woman told me she stopped in Damascus to buy vases for her new place in peaceful Amman. She'd had enough of the fifteen-year war in Lebanon and was relocating. Several other passengers agreed that the train was their road from war to peace.

When I hitched through the region, Britain's Lawrence and his First World War exploits were long dead. But tremors from that war were still felt among the nations and peoples that emerged from the rubble. The scenery hadn't changed much, except for all the pick-ups that replaced camels in Bedouin camps scattered throughout the desert. Black basalt rocks, the residue of volcanic eruptions long ago, remained to tell their stories of Romans, Greeks, Persians, and Turks who lingered among the local Arabs. Those were stories I could only imagine, but what's an imagination for?

As the engine, a faded green and yellow, jerked the train from its post in Damascus, children jumped on and off, playing their own hitching game. I doubted that children played that game in 1908. At the other end of the run Jordanian children snatched coins from the track to examine how the train wheels had warped the coins. Kids probably didn't have spare change in 1908. Passports in hand, passengers who had abandoned Lebanon were lining up to kiss Amman hello. I wondered.... Would the forty-minute flight from Damascus to Amman, with other foreigners like me, local sheikhs and elites, have taught me as much about the people, the land, the past and present, as a cheap hitch on a train that had all the speed and comfort of a stagecoach?

OO

When I arrived in the city of Sofia, she greeted me kindly despite her embarrassing home life. Her kindness was trickery because her real life was broken like shattered glass. Her dress was tattered, her rouge streaked and smeared, her table scant. Her abandoned pets raged through the streets sniffing for bits of fat or sinew, alive or dead. Dinner, one decent meal, in Sofia's finest cost as much as an entire apartment had a few years earlier. In the mid-nineties, her currency, the lev, lost much of its vanishing value by the hour. Capitalism's value was still much in doubt. Fast food at American chain restaurants was almost free. But if your pockets were empty, paying less than seven cents for a hamburger and fifteen or sixteen cents for a soda was too much. Too many bad people operated from the shadows. Too few good people were visible and in power. Most of the population was left feeling helpless and overwhelmed by unseen forces arrayed against them. Official corruption at the top made the transition from stagnant communism to wobbly capitalism ragged and dubious. Billions were drained from the government and the little people. Huge foreign and domestic debts led to raging inflation, and the banking system, absent needed reforms, flopped.

When I stumbled on Sofia's embarrassment of poverty my intention was merely to find a trail through Bulgaria to Belgrade, Serbia's capital and the core of the Bosnian wars. Long stymied in my many attempts to wrangle a Serbian visa, I got lucky in Sofia. Commingled with my unveiling of Sofia's plight, and the Serbian visa stuffed in my pocket, I booked an unexpected but fascinating train ride with smugglers. On the road for me, this was a true threefer.

Believe it or not, Sofia was doing its best to impress me as it clawed into the light from the long, dark Communist era. At the same time, Bulgaria's capital lacked the means to be as embracing as Woonsocket was in welcoming the permanence of my grandparents and their cousins almost a century earlier on another continent.

Though a national capital, Sofia was a side-hitch for me. As I loitered and learned her story, the city and Bulgaria itself served as the gateway to a bigger prize, Belgrade. For me Belgrade was a gray city that existed only in shadows because I had never been able to get a visa to visit the country. Sofia opened the door to Belgrade. A railroad, the Balkan Express, would chug me through that open door.

A most inexpensive but elaborate lunch in a fine restaurant led to a conversation with a person who had a connection in the Yugoslav/Serbian embassy. The connection knew the path to the visa that I wanted, so I paid up to help at least one person in Sofia's economy. Before Sofia's hungry, rampaging hounds could sniff me on a side street, I bought a train ticket to Belgrade and left Sofia to her wits before anyone knew we were pals.

Just before I fled Sofia in late November, I bought grub for the journey: dense wheat bread, cheese, bottled water, and packaged meat. Blindly, I trusted the bakers, the butchers and the cheese-makers. My trust was soon rewarded as I learned once more that food is an international lubricant for getting a story. In this case food was magical.

Soon after I located my frigid first class cabin, three women strolled happily into what I believed was my exclusive suite. They were smugglers, not of drugs, rifles, or explosives, but of clothes. The husband of one of the women quickly claimed special status and moved in. He, too, was a smuggler, transporting clothes, mostly shirts, lots of shirts. Smuggling was an art form for this gang of four, and giggling was their introductory act. Act Two followed when they stripped down to thin short-sleeve shirts, which swelled my wonder and interest. In Act Three they cracked open their overstuffed luggage bags and removed all the long knitted jerseys and shirts that they would yank on, layer after layer, under their heavy winter coats. During Act Four the smugglers took turns pummeling their coats and extra garments underneath to smooth and round out their disguise and make them look like ordinary, though overweight, travelers.

Then came Intermission, which was of great interest to me.

During that pause, the uninvited guests in my suite added to our menu more bottled water, olives, cheese, two loaves of bread and extra meat that resembled kielbasa, along with a precious knife to slice the cheese and make sandwiches. The women spread the food on our first-class table with great glee. I kicked my contribution into the buffet and we shared it all. We ate; I asked questions. We ate, and they answered. The more we ate the more the Bulgarians — well oiled with a little protein, carbs, and respect from a foreigner who respected them and their trade — volunteered information about their smuggling ventures, and their profits. They had a great story to tell; I listened and made notes. Their human story, without any gore, was a great surprise. I never expected to hear a tale told by Bulgarian smugglers on a train to Belgrade, where I didn't think the door would ever open to me.

During and after lunch, the smugglers told of their twice-weekly moneymaking enterprise that linked Bulgarians and Serbs. With all the instruments of note taking at my command, plus sign language, a map and a Bulgarian dictionary, their story sparkled as part of my hitchhiking history. To this day, and for that reason, my smugglers' lunch remains one of the best I've ever had anywhere. Dessert, for me only, was my ticket all the way to Belgrade. In their Final Act, the smugglers drifted through Serbian customs without a hitch. Why not? They were steady customers, so their obvious bulk was ignored. The Bulgarian smugglers needed cash, and their Serbian customers needed clothes: no harm, no foul.

Suitably disguised and fed, the smugglers and their merchandise would proceed undetected into Serbia. I rode deeper into Serbia, all the way to Belgrade.

Because of the company I kept and the story I learned, lunch on the Balkan Express, minus an official dining car, outranked dinner on a twenty-four hour train ride through Russia's great northern forests from Archangel to St. Petersburg a few years later. To get the attention of the chef from Azerbaijan on that endless ride, and because chickens speak a universal language, I clucked loudly and flapped my arms, hoping that the chef would catch the clue. The knowing chef laughed and pointed to his thigh and chest, meaning leg or breast. Both, I answered, holding up two fingers and pointing to my leg and my chest. The chef laughed again, louder.

OO

Surrounded by people eager to catch the Zephyr that was long past its scheduled arrival time, I might as well have been standing alone in the Sahara. No one would talk to me, a stranger heading south just as they were. Passengers shuffling in place on Platform One in Skopje's dreary Central Station preferred silence and a snack pulled from a pocket. Maybe they thought I was a Greek intelligence officer or something. In most places I knew from experience, I could pass for a local or a neighbor. Sometimes that was helpful. Sometimes not so much, and this was one of those not-so-much moments. The train would be bound for Athens. But at the time Macedonians weren't allowed to enter Greece. Why, the other passengers may have thought, take a chance and get caught talking to a Greek? This problem between Greece and Macedonia wasn't personal or rational. It was all about nationalism or national ego on Greece's part, and Macedonia's new name, then the Former Yugoslav Republic of Macedonia (FYROM). Greece, after all, claimed that it and it alone owned the name Macedonia. I didn't need more locals to underline Macedonia's existential anxieties, which were already in my notebook. Serbia and Kosovo and the prospect of a real war hovered in the north. With Greece to the south, the nettles were historical and geographic, more about names and flags than bullets and bombs.

The train from Budapest to Belgrade reached Skopje two hours and fifteen minutes late. No wonder the people waiting in Skopje were so anxious. Belgrade is in Serbia, the main provocateur of the Bosnian wars. From Skopje the Zephyr would skim overnight in time to catch a televised soccer game at the Greek border before rumbling into Athens, ready to break the fast for yoghurt, fresh bread, an omelet, olives, tomatoes and sausages.

This hitching excursion was another occasion when I learned more by osmosis than by active engagement, more by just showing up than by meeting prime ministers or princes. Macedonians in Skopje, for example, were allowed to sell me, an American, a basic ticket for $34.50 to ride all the way to Athens. But only a Greek conductor could sell me an additional $18 ticket for the right to occupy my own sleeper compartment, which was too sweet a deal to pass up. When I gave the Greek conductor a $20 bill, he was embarrassed because, he said, he didn't have enough money to make change. Where have I heard that story before? I thought. When I told him to keep the $2 and buy a little Ouzo at lunch, the conductor laughed and apologized repeatedly because the train was old and dirty, and the light in my sleeper didn't work. In his slippers, T-shirt and gray slacks that missed the Deep Clean cycle, the conductor looked more like a poor baggage handler than a man of conductor status.

Shortly after we pulled away from Platform One, a woman wielding a broom swept through the train but missed my cabin. I didn't call her to return, but she did anyway, not to sweep but to deliver a baby pillow, a blanket and a sheet that also missed the Deep Clean cycle. The moment was the last week of August in 1995. In a word, sultry would describe the hour shortly after 7 p.m., when we left Skopje. My cabin was hot. To admit air, I had to lower the window and raise the shade. But when the train moved and wobbled, the window and shade went in the wrong directions. No air. After midnight I quit the window-shade fight and slept through the heat with my baby pillow and sheet. The blanket wasn't necessary.

As a kid, I never rode into or out of Woonsocket on a train. Even without that experience, I knew intuitively that the Woonsocket to Providence special would have surpassed in speed and comfort my train travels in the Balkans and the Middle East.

Traveling solo overnight to Athens in my heated cabin when heat wasn't needed reminded me of an earlier overnight train ride from Moscow to Leningrad, now called St. Petersburg again. That was in 1990. Riding the rails north on that trip I wasn't alone, being compelled to share a sleeper with another person, a middle-aged man named Simon. Most of that night, I stayed awake, listening to Simon tell me his woes in the midst of the Soviet Union's collapse. Simon would no longer be needed because his job was eliminated. A cog in the bureaucracy, Simon's task was to plan the future of Soviet society, which he did diligently. Until, that is, Simon and the rest of the world learned that there would be no future Soviet society. Simon was looking for a way out, aiming for Israel. I never learned whether Simon reached the beaches of Tel Aviv or an Israeli settlement in the Palestinian West Bank. Five years later, as I thought of Simon, all I knew was that I was headed south on the Zephyr and would be allowed to reach Athens because I wasn't a Macedonian.

When the Zephyr reached the Greek border, two hours and fifteen minutes after we left Skopje, almost all the passengers walked away. As an American, I was allowed to stay aboard. Everyone knew the rules. After my passport was checked and returned, we left the border, but not before we watched a soccer match on television for half an hour. Locals drank beer and listened to the night noise serenade the otherwise vacant neighborhood.

Dawn brought farms and hills tucked in valleys and sprinklers watering fields of vegetables. Sheep and goats grazed unknowing that I was snug in my cabin with no air. We reached Athens at 9:22 a.m., only two hours and twenty-two minutes late, which meant that we hadn't lost more travel time to the soccer match. Only two other passengers left the train in Athens, meaning they weren't Macedonians either. Greeks and Macedonians, especially the Greeks, wanted me and other outsiders to understand how politics in the Balkans worked. I already knew, but hitching on the Zephyr leavened my knowledge.

McCarthy's Department Store, Downtown Woonsocket

Woonsocket Train

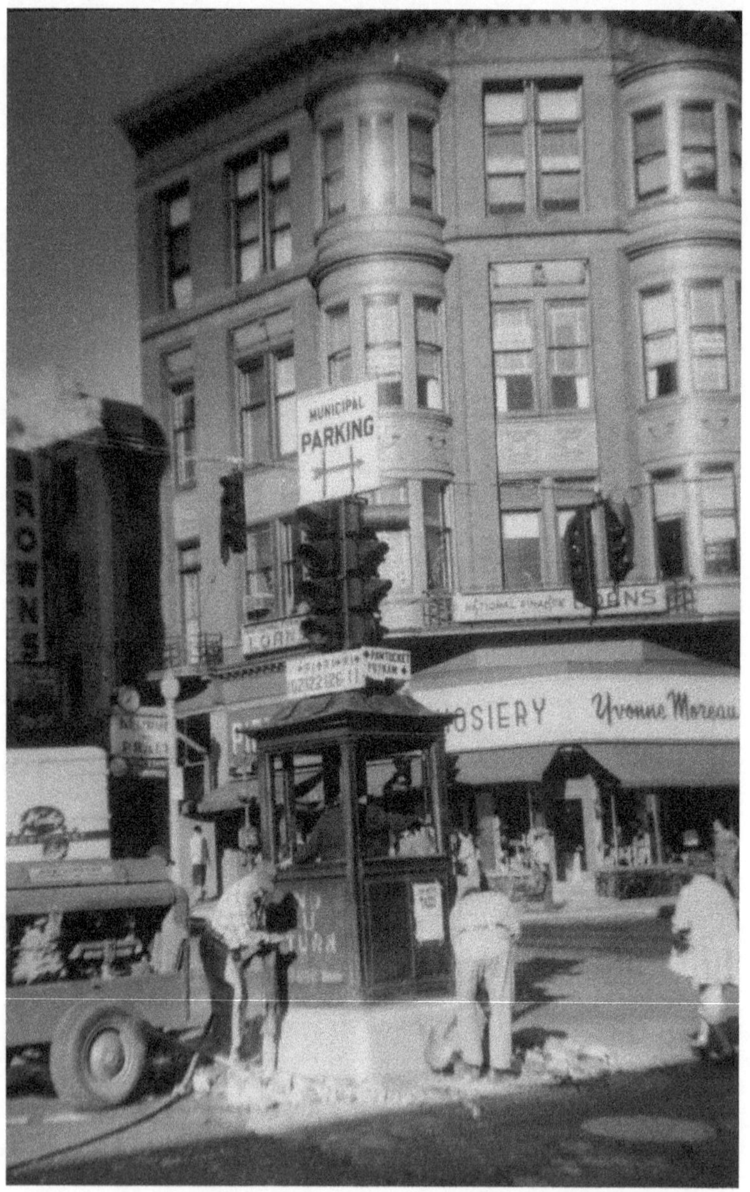

Downtown Woonsocket, MA., circa 1950

Hejaz Railway Station, Damascus
By Heretiq - Own work, CC BY-SA 3.0

KOSOVO
ALBANIA
MACEDONIA
*Fier
*Vlore
*Gjirocaster
*Saranda
GREECE
*Ioannina

11 | ALBANIA – CLIMBING A PYRAMID

Mist hugged the earth and haze shrouded the snowy peaks on the morning I rolled into angry Albania. The road was wide open and so was the border as ethnic Greeks and Albanians were fleeing because Albania was in the blooming stages of a national uprising. Popular anger was focused on a president universally believed to have led Ponzi schemes that cost many Albanians dearly. Raids on army barracks and police stations reflected Everyman's anger over their loss of cash and faith, a result of their investments in what are popularly known as pyramid schemes. Havoc raced through the small mountainous country with the speed of robbers stripping banks in lawless towns. Albania was struggling to emerge from decades of dictatorship and alien allegiances that morphed from early Yugoslav solidarity to Soviet-style communism before the country's dictator embraced the Maoist brand. As the country slipped down that rabbit hole, Albanians became trapped by ignorance and paranoia that fed blind obedience, victims of an archaic formula that punished them for too long.

By early March 1997, when my time to cross Albania's open border had come, I was well schooled in the art and science of hitchhiking. In the late Fifties, I had bummed my way through two years of college decades before I widened my horizons by hitching in Aleppo, along an old Silk Road from Turkey into Iraq, in Moscow, Somalia, and other overheated climate zones too numerous to repeat. When I hurried north to the border at

Qafë Botë - Sagiada, I didn't have a visa; I hadn't even tried to buy one, over or under the table. The solitary border boss waved me in without a word, never mind a question. Many others, all fleeing south to Greece, left as though they wouldn't be going back. On subsequent days, the border boss had left to go fishing. The border fence was wide open. Busy battling among themselves, Albanians couldn't waste time policing a border. The borderless border made it easy for me to hustle for more than a week in and out of Albania as if I were an Albanian or a Greek leaving to save my life or go shopping. Neither shopper nor tourist, I was an American newspaperman searching for details about the national uproar. Albanians couldn't tell me their stories fast enough.

To reach the Greek-Albanian border, I took a jammed Olympic Air twin-engine prop from Athens to Ioannina, as beautiful a Greek town as I expected a Greek town to be. The flight lasted one hour and ten minutes. The drive from Ioannina to the Albanian border took an hour and thirty minutes. In Ioannina I kept a room at the Hotel Zenia. Every two or three days I returned to that room to file stories. This is where Geni entered my story. Geni, who was truly a genie, was my driver. Without Geni I might have stumbled around useless checkpoints and bumbled past penniless Albanians who wanted to tell me all about their pain.

Because my journey throughout the uprising didn't stop until I returned to Athens, it was as if I had never arrived in Albania. Geni and I drove around the small mountainous country, very much a part of the Balkans, which itself means mountains. We scurried through valleys and over mountains in Geni's dust-colored Mercedes, which was too old to have been newly stolen and too new to have been pilfered during the country's darkest days of dictatorship. Geni and I sought information that struck us head on in every village, town, and small city, where each checkpoint was more an invitation to pass than a barrier to prevent our passing. I was, after all, in Albania to tell the people's story, and the people couldn't stop talking.

Checkpoints littered every road. Yet for Geni and me the checkpoints were nowhere because they weren't barriers and served no purpose beyond high and low drama. Newly armed kids never threatened us. The checkpoints were naked of any shakedowns, although the newly armed could have used donations. Donkey carts, trash bins, and kitchen sinks masked as checkpoints served more as expressions of anger and sudden freedom than as barriers to me or anyone else. Mental images of revolutions past made the Albanian model seem like it was lifted from a booklet that ordered junior rebels to establish checkpoints and raid arms depots while their leaders took over radio stations and airports. The only parts my hosts got right were the silly checkpoints and the raids on police stations and army depots.

As easily as Geni's Mercedes rolled through checkpoints in third gear, we found teachers, construction workers, and army colonels – people of every class and caste – eager to rant about the tens of thousands of dollars they lost to ten pyramid schemes allegedly backed by Albania's president Sali Berisha, a cardiologist. Albanians weren't the first suckers seeking easy profits from fraudulent chain schemes, and they won't be anywhere near the last. A Ponzi, or pyramid, scheme lures new investors to pay the huge profits that were promised to earlier investors; the pyramid collapses when new investors dwindle or disappear entirely, and promised profits can no longer be paid to any dreamer.

Every man, woman and child wielding a weapon believed that Berisha and/or his political party had doctored their money, leaving them more impoverished than ever. Investors, suckered into the schemes because they sought a quick exit from decades of poverty, said they were promised a 300 percent profit on their investments. Instead, they lost the principal, most of which they were certain went straight up the ladder to Albania's political elite or simply disappeared. The largest pyramid scheme, I learned, lured $800 million from investors who had lost it all. Geni, who drove me through and around fake checkpoints, swore that he was too poor to be taken in by promises of earning 300 percent interest on his investment.

With the help of people we interviewed, Geni assured me that Berisha, not an American journalist, was the main target of popular anger. Newly armed teen-agers and their parents never stopped shouting about how Berisha had tricked them. No one bragged about how many people the rebels had killed, though there weren't many. At the same time, people complained that rebels were killing rebels, mostly by accident and by raining bullets down upon themselves. In some towns, rebels and residents sheltered young, innocent army soldiers from harm. In one town, rebels disarmed and stripped soldiers of their weapons and clothing before releasing them naked into the mountains. That story sounded as if it were lifted straight out of classical Greek mythology. The government wasn't fighting back; to the rebels the fight was personal, against Berisha but no one else. On a global scale, the uprising didn't rise to the level of a carnival test where a strongman tries to whack a lever hard enough to propel a hockey puck skyward to bang a bell.

In Vlorë, a seaside town where the uprising began, Geni and I wormed through a roadblock made of kitchen sinks and car mufflers. Unlike clan crossings in Somalia, no one demanded cash to cross. Donkey carts and burned trucks formed another barrier, where kids jokingly asked for ten American dollars to pass. No money exchanged hands because I feared being accused of contributing to the delinquency of minors. Off to the side of the road near Gjirocaster, the hometown of long-dead, longtime dictator Enver Hoxha, I watched a man show a woman how to shoot a handgun. No one was killed or wounded during that lesson.

Off to the side of one checkpoint, a man said of Berisha, "At first he steals our votes; after that he steals our money; now we can't give our lives."

Panu Gicali, a dentist in Sarandä, said "There are two ways out: the way of blood or the way of democracy. There is no other way." Rebels drove cars once owned by the police and played soldier on tanks that belonged to the army.

At a checkpoint in Vlorë, sixteen-year-old kids were firing away at random with guns they took from soldiers and cops. But Geni and I had no problems. He knew the neighborhood; Geni knew that being charged with loitering was our greatest threat.

"Show me your press card," a kid said in a language I didn't understand. But Geni understood, and even Geni laughed. Geni knew I had no Albanian press card because none existed. The kid was manning a sink, two car mufflers, and a tree limb that posed as a gate at a checkpoint by the Seman River at the industrial town of Fier.

"Show me your passport," Geni said, relaying the kid's second demand. A passport was new to the kid's eyes; the kid just wanted to eye one. No one asked for my visa; maybe they knew better. But Fier itself was stable and relatively calm. An army base was abandoned, its weapons stolen with no reprisals.

On the road from Fier to Berat, we passed an oil field with derricks still pumping. An oil field in Albania was a surprising vision.

At another faux checkpoint near Berat, a beautiful town at the foot of mountains topped with snow and with a river running through the valley, bathtubs, trash bins, and a stick between them formed what was supposed to look like a gate. The barrier looked like a railroad crossing in an impoverished town; kids, smiling, raised the stick between the bathtubs and the trash bins to open the road.

This hitch was easy because I rode with Geni in his Mercedes. Geni knew his people and was sympathetic to all because he understood the pressures of poverty. He mocked no one.

The uprising began when police attacked student protesters in Vlorë on the Adriatic. Soon, forty-five students were on a hunger strike for eleven days in Gjirocaster. From the moment I entered Albania, it was clear the revolt was disorganized. It was effective, however, probably because the country itself was disorganized. The revolt rippled from the bottom up. If there was top-down leadership, I missed it, and it missed me. From where I sat, the uprising was a town-to-town affair, with no cohesion. At the same time, the people understood the reason that kids and women joined men in seizing army and police posts and demanded the return of their investments.

Bashkim Lamaj summarized the uprising, a story many others repeated. Lamaj said he worked in construction in Italy for three years and saved $40,000, all of which he invested, and lost, in one pyramid scheme.

"Albania is not a big bingo game," he said. "I lost my house."

Lamaj was 42 years old when we spoke, with a wife and two children. Some people, he said, took out loans from the government via the European Union to buy tractors for their farms, then sold the tractors to get money to invest in the pyramid schemes. When we spoke, Lamaj said he was the chief of extension services in Albania's Agriculture Department. He earned $100 a month in his state job. A bit of a poet and philosopher, he said, "The worst enemy is cruelty."

The Osumi River flowed through Berat, whose historic old quarter is protected by the United Nations Educational, Scientific and Cultural Organization. Fuzzy cheeked gunmen looted army bases and set up new checkpoints that were as porous as all the others that Geni and I crossed. Throughout the south, rebels chopped down trees in attempts to block roads. In the village of Grajica, three women hoed in a field as men rushed to protect them against false reports that soldiers were on the way to attack women in the village. One kid used a piece of rope to sling his new rifle over his shoulder.

On the road between Vlorë and Sarandë, telephone lines were strung on broken tree limbs stuck in the ground. They posed as a checkpoint. Some of the limbs looked like scarecrows; others looked like simple arms and legs sticking only a few feet above the earth. One person, reportedly hired by the government to counter the rebels, tossed a grenade from a car. Before the grenade exploded a rebel snatched it out of the air and hurled it back at the car where the original grenade-thrower was killed in the ensuing blast, while three others escaped harm.

After I interviewed enough Albanians to learn the size of the pyramid schemes and their damage, and counted the weapons looted from soldiers and cops, I left Albania as I had entered. Crossing back into Greece a final time proved as easy as driving through Albania. No one was on duty at the border, not even to extract a little extortion. Geni and I said goodbye at the visa-free border, and I hitched a ride to the Hotel Zenia. With seven others, I was on a waiting list for a flight to the Greek capital. Without having to pay a middleman for a ticket, I beat the odds and boarded another twin-engine Olympic Air prop bound for Athens. At the Associated Press office there, I filed more stories and shipped photos to my office in Washington. With a visa or without, I've had countless difficulties entering and leaving a country. Nowhere was the process easier than it was at Albania's border with Greece.

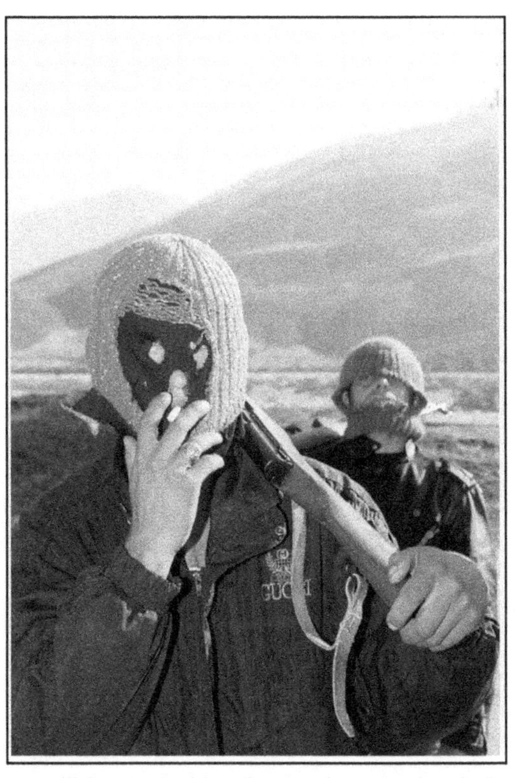

Albanian militiamen hold a checkpoint, South of Tirana, during the Albanian Pyramid Crisis (1997)
Mark H. Milstein/ Northfoto

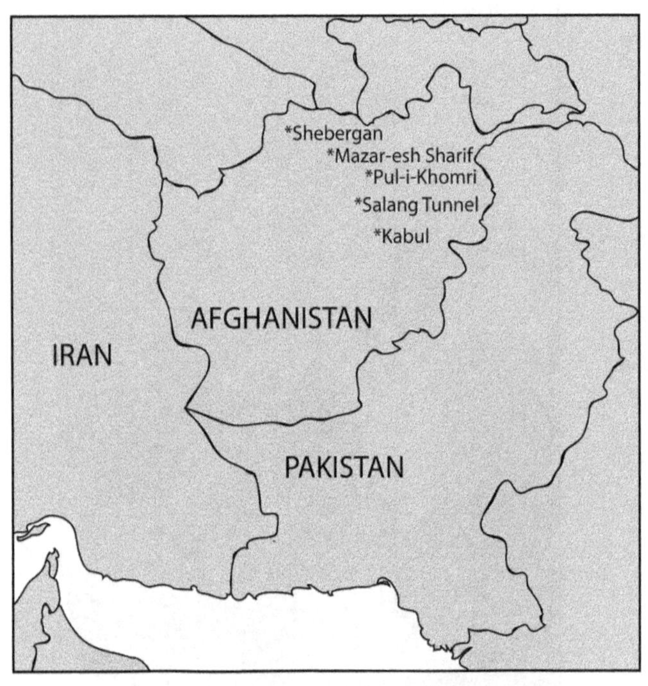
*Shebergan
*Mazar-esh Sharif
*Pul-i-Khomri
*Salang Tunnel
*Kabul
AFGHANISTAN
IRAN
PAKISTAN

12 | ROAD WARRIOR

Four cars were floating in two small ponds. Even in Afghanistan that was weird. Worse, the ponds, the cars and the people who had ridden in them were in a dangerous mountain tunnel. "Warning. Danger of Poisoning in the Tunnel." Those words greeted all who entered the Salang Tunnel in the Hindu Kush Mountains, fifty-six miles northwest of Kabul.

If I hadn't known when we stopped to put chains on our tires and to rescue two colleagues whose car was snowbound, I knew it when I read the warning sign: this would be nothing like hitchhiking to college.

Asphyxiation inside the tunnel wasn't the only danger. Avalanches were poised like arrows to zap motorists stuck in a blizzard while waiting to enter the 1.6 mile-long-tunnel. The prospect of spending days, cold and hungry, trapped at the tunnel's entrance without being able to execute a U-turn turned many a would-be traveler into a coward. Once inside the tunnel, motorists abandoned their cars and fled on foot to avoid carbon monoxide poisoning. Others pushed cars spinning in foot-deep ice ruts to open the one-lane road. To save themselves, people were forced to help save others. Cars that failed to wade through ponds formed by melted snow stayed in place, maybe until summer.

Twenty-three feet high and the same width, the Salang Tunnel is more than two miles above sea level. That's high, not so high as to be in the death zone but it's a bother that can be felt in the bones. Factor in the biting cold and the carbon monoxide, and the trouble becomes mental as well as physical. Outside the tunnel, the air wasn't poisonous, but it was thin; rarefied is the usual term. The Salang wasn't a mausoleum, but many people have died inside its tomb-like confines.

On the road from the Afghan capital northwest to the city of Mazar-esh-Sharif the dangers, if not immediately as lethal as those in the Salang Tunnel, multiplied. Broken asphalt and deep snow clogged the trail leading to a series of smaller tunnels and shaky bridges. Together, they posed their own risks before the Salang spelled out "Danger of Poisoning." From day to day, traffic in the tunnel alternated in different directions. On a given day, only northbound traffic was permitted. On the following day, only traffic heading south was allowed. At either end of the Salang, the dramatic crush of cars morphed into two or three lanes as cars and trucks all competed to enter the single-lane tunnel. Instantly, the vehicles formed a demolition derby like no other I'd seen, though the speeds were slower.

In the weeks and months following the American invasion, the Students of Islam — known as the Taliban — were on the run, but other tribal chiefs vied for money and power. Wars, without bullets but just as dangerous, awaited travelers who ventured in vehicles across friendless deserts, around or through mountains imprisoned by snow and ice.

War of the roads, I called those combat-like conditions. Cars broke down as often as they did not. Oil leaks and broken fan belts disabled vehicles as though shot through the heart. Chains snapped where they were wrapped around tires to help grind through ice, shifting autos automatically into neutral.

On this trip my target was Abdul Rashid Dostum, an ethnic-

Uzbek military commander and political figure of a high order and shifting allegiances in Afghanistan. Most of what transpired on the road in search of Dostum was incidental, though not without consequence. Dostum was the country's deputy defense minister, a person of great interest at the time. He became vice president in 2014, though I missed his inauguration. In 2001, the year before Uncle Sam's invasion, Dostum was a major American ally in the big fight against the Taliban, and he remained a figure of great controversy. He had fought with Afghan communists during the Soviet invasion in the 1980s, then switched sides to battle the Soviets before he fought against the Taliban in the civil war, and followed that by fighting with the American forces against the Taliban. Dostum's stronghold was in Sheberghān, a city eighty miles west of the larger city of Mazar-esh-Sharif, known locally as Mazar. My intelligence reported that I could interview Dostum at his compound in Sheberghān. My intelligence wasn't intelligent enough.

OO

Shawfiq's watch alarm beeped at 4:15 a.m. It was March 30, 2002. I rented a room in the house that Shawfiq managed in Kabul, and we both knew that the alarm was the signal for me to hit the road, the ice and snow, the frightful tunnel, and all 372 miles to Mazar-esh-Sharif. Depending on the weather and the crush of cars, Eymal, Abdullah and Assaf — my scouts and general factotums — all agreed, the journey could take from twelve to twenty-four hours. Figure twenty four hours, I mumbled. But we didn't beat the worst odds, reaching Mazar more than twenty-four hours after I left Shawfiq with my three helpers in Assaf's old eight-passenger Toyota Town Ace van. Our speed would register a few ticks more than twenty miles per hour. The good news was that we were heading north on a day when northbound traffic through the Salang was permitted. One misinformed news reporter I knew had attempted to travel north from Kabul on a day when only southbound traffic was permitted. His trip took more than two days because he was forced to return to Kabul overnight before heading north again the following day.

Immediately, I knew this journey would render as routine mine of forty-four years earlier. Those were my days of waiting at 7:15 a.m. Eastern Standard Time at Millville's flashing yellow light in 1958 for Dickie McCrohan or Mr. Berkowicz to drive me seven miles to Uxbridge on the first leg of my daily hitch to college. Dickie McCrohan or Mr. Berkowitz got me started in 1958. Eymal, Abdullah and Assaf and Assaf's old van were my safety net in 2002.

Eymal's, Abdullah's and Assaf's watch alarms were in sync with Shawfiq's. The trio reached me on schedule. Assaf drove the four of us to the house of a man named Mustafa. Mustafa, with a friend along for the joy ride, drove another news reporter, a news photographer and their gear in his small truck. After delays to acquire more film and fill his truck with gas, Mustafa and company tailed us through roads steeped in snow and ice, and with visibility that at times was almost nil. Those weather warnings told Assaf to stop and attach chains before we entered one of several small tunnels on the way to the monster tunnel. Mustafa followed suit, attaching chains to the rear tires of his smaller vehicle. Like a limping wagon train, our large van and Mustafa's small truck stayed close as we approached the main tunnel. That's when the chains on Mustafa's truck snapped. So long, Mustafa. When Assaf realized that we had lost Mustafa, Eymal, my translator, and I walked back to find him and his two passengers. Eymal and I helped the other American reporter and photographer haul their gear half a mile to Assaf's van so they wouldn't be stranded. We didn't see Mustafa and his truck again for two days, when he finally reached Mazar.

Eymal, our two new passengers, and I plodded through deep snow and slush to reach our slow moving van. Loading the additional passengers and their equipment was easy because our van had extra cargo space in the rear. A single-car wagon train, we plowed on, slowly but not for long before bedlam greeted us at the tunnel's entrance. A blizzard was roaring, horns were honking, and two or three lines of cars were attempting to squeeze into the entrance of the blocked tunnel that had only one lane. More complications greeted us when some drivers stopped to help others snap on chains. In the blinding snow, truly a whiteout, freezing temperatures and deafening noise, one Afghan truck driver stood out in sandals and traditional cotton garments insisting that he wasn't cold. Bundled like a Nanook of the North, I stood humbly interviewing the iceman.

Two hours after we had reached the entrance, we entered the Salang Tunnel, a van with six passengers, much equipment, chains still in place, and big hopes of surviving the crossing. Abdullah, a man we journalists call a fixer because he's adept at arranging interviews with strangers, and Assaf pushed cars through the snow, slush and ponds to open the road. After a two-hour delay inside the tunnel, we inhaled fresh air. The other reporter and photographer left the van and walked through the tunnel to escape possible poisoning. Many stalled motorists, including us, turned off their engines to reduce the poison in the air while we waited for the road to be cleared. I stayed in the van with Eymal. The entire scene had the aura of a miracle because we made it through, two hours and six minutes after we had entered the tunnel of our nightmares.

Darkness closed in rapidly after we left the poisonous tunnel. Traveling at night, on what were mostly roads in name only in alien territory, is never a bright idea, so overnight found us in a hospitable guest house in a town two hours north of the Salang Tunnel. Our quarters were more than decent, as was the food.

Not long after sunrise, we were bound for Mazar.

Mazar-ash-Sharif, a pleasant city, counts ethnic Uzbeks, Tajiks and Turkmen among its half a million residents. Mazar is home to the large and beautiful Shrine of Haznet Ali, also called The Blue Mosque.

Mazar's surprises were far warmer and smoother than the road through the mountains and its tunnels. Our entourage walked unannounced into a movie premier, an historic, homemade film of Afghanistan's forgotten past that even featured star-crossed lovers. Under Taliban control the movie would have been banned forever.

Well after midnight our band caught a few winks at a small hotel, easily the best I eyed in more than a week in northern Afghanistan, or in more than a month in the entire country. Just after daylight we were on another rough road, though one without tunnels or mountains of snow, aiming for the city of Sheberghān, in the high steppes not far from the borders with Uzbekistan and Turkmenistan. We were after Dostum, the military and political leader who knew much about Afghanistan's turbulent present, and of its civil war that led to the Taliban's rise. Dostum might even have information about Osama Bin Laden, the mastermind of the September 11, 2001 attacks in New York and Washington. Bin Laden had been sheltered in

Afghanistan, and the American military wanted him badly. Not until May of 2011 did American forces find and kill Bin Laden in neighboring Pakistan. Their hunt ended after nearly ten years on the trail. I didn't have that much time.

After a two-and-a-half-hour drive to Sheberghān, we reached Dostum's cloister. Two more news reporters and their translator were finishing lunch when all six of our clan walked in on them and Dostum's peacocks that were screeching outside. We made it in time for lunch, but that was all. Dostum wasn't within sight or earshot.

An aide to the Uzbek chief promised that his boss would meet us the following morning in Mazar. That was the Afghan way of telling us to get lost. I asked whether we could do a sleepover, and stay for dinner at the compound where we had a satisfying lunch. No one laughed except me. The Uzbek chief ducked us. We never met him.

Our luck in the automotive world was holding, but it wouldn't last. Assaf sniffed the problem. A young mechanic nearby diagnosed the illness. An oil leak was about to gum up the works. On the edge of Sheberghān, directed by a kid mechanic, Assaf drove over a hole in the ground. In any language, that hole was the equivalent of a lift. The mechanic scrambled down into the hole, examined the engine and told Assaf what Assaf already knew: the engine was leaking oil. "Too many bad roads and poisonous tunnels," I said to Assaf. He nodded.

There I was, in 2002, stuck in an Afghan desert with an ailing car. I'd been in a similar predicament before, back in Millville, Massachusetts in the late 1950s, driving a green, two-door 1950 Ford sedan that was ailing with a leaky master cylinder and a less than efficient flywheel. Rudy, my erstwhile mechanical genius, pointed me toward cheap solutions. Sometimes Rudy asked me to drive over the hole in the ground, his lift, at his shop so he could change the oil. Rudy's larger hole in the ground had steps; the small hole in Sheberghān's earth had no steps; the young mechanic simply jumped in before our van drove over him so he could examine the oil leak.

We decided to head back to Mazar after Assaf poured what he called diesel oil into the engine.

"Don't worry," Assaf said, "I can buy more oil and we can make it to Mazar, and fix it in the morning." We kicked the oilcan down the road and drove back to Mazar. The road was so bad along the way that Assaf drove off what remained of the asphalt and into the dirt to preserve his leaking engine. Assaf narrowly missed a van full of humans and one large pelican propped up in the rear seat. Only I thought that the pelican passenger was odd.

Assaf kept his promise the next morning. The oil leak was repaired. Dostum didn't keep his promise, or at least his aide didn't. Before noon we were sailing back to Sheberghān from Mazar. Proud that his engine could hold oil without leaking, Assaf sped past a horse-drawn cart pulling a car without mechanical brakes while a man held a rope attached to the rear bumper of the car to provide the "hand" brakes. That contraption, I was certain, would never make it through the Salang Tunnel. No one thought the sight worth a word. There was, at least, no chance that this car, without brakes of its own, would have a leaky master cylinder like my 1950 Ford.

Outside the ruins of the ancient imperial capital of Balkh, woe struck again. The fan belt snapped and we were stuck in a desert once more, at a spot where, I was reassured, people in three cars had been robbed the previous night.

"No problem," Assaf assured me, as rain hammered the van, "I will find a ride (hitchhike) back to Mazar and bring back a new belt. You wait."

Abdullah, Eymal and I waited because our choices were limited. By this time, Mustafa had caught up to us earlier in Mazar and snatched his own original two passengers from our van. But we weren't alone waiting for Assaf to return with a fan belt. Two young boys heading into what looked like a worse storm back home in Uzbekistan sought shelter in our van. We all shared Meals Ready To Eat, courtesy of the American military and American taxpayers. The boys taught me to count from one to twenty in Dari, the Afghan dialect of the Persian Farsi, and I taught them to say their numbers in English.

An Afghan hitchhiking in Afghanistan to help me was a twist in my story. To begin with, auto traffic in the desert isn't what anyone would call heavy. But hitchhiking there is easy. Assaf simply stood by the roadside and waved his arms as the first car approached. Presto! The car stopped and Assaf was off to Mazar to find a fan belt.

Two hours later, Assaf returned with a teen-age mechanic who went right to work on the engine that was hidden under the passenger side of the front seat. Assaf had hitched a ride back into the desert to rescue us and his van. The mechanic was the same one who had repaired the oil leak earlier that same day in Mazar. Mirwis was the mechanic's name. Mirwis was, he said, sixteen, and had been working on cars for five years. He might, I thought, be another Rudy.

A sand storm began kicking up when Mirwis discovered a radiator leak. Why not? Radiators don't like eighteen-hour journeys on washboard roads and demolition derbies at the entrance to a tunnel filled with carbon monoxide. Mirwis was no rookie repairman. He knew the landscape and the possible troubles. Mirwis pulled a tube of radiator sealer from his pants pocket and, presto, the radiator held water and we were off again. Assaf was spared a second hitch to Mazar and back carrying radiator sealer in his pocket.

Well into the second day of what was to be a day trip to the city of Sheberghān, a deluge struck as we approached my new target, a desert prison stuffed with all the usual suspects, famished young men wearing little clothing and just as little fat under their skin, and most bearing a religious bent. Prison doctors told me the small cells were choked with 2,700 prisoners, double the prison's capacity. Those I interviewed said they had been rounded up by the Taliban and forced to fight the invading Americans and their Afghan allies. Most of the prisoners were from Afghanistan and Pakistan. Others had joined the jihad, the holy war, from Uzbekistan, Saudi Arabia, China, Libya, Yemen and Tajikistan; many of those were bound for the American prison at Guantanamo, Cuba, though they didn't know it then.

The region of Sheberghān had been the scene of great killing the year before I arrived. The story is the same wherever war rules. By definition and execution, war itself is a war crime. No need to quibble over diplomatic definitions. Whether wrongly started or rightly countered, in war innocent civilians suffer the most.

When I returned from the prison to Assaf's van, the ever-resourceful Mirwis reported that he had replaced a fraying engine belt with one he had stuffed in his pocket back in Mazar. Just in case, said Mirwis, who knew his business.

My war with the roads and failing auto parts was unending. All the roads in Afghanistan were the same: bad and worse. Old autos were the same, old. The mechanics who replaced the broken auto parts and the people who fetched the mechanics, however, were Grade-A. The main road out of town and country from Kabul east to the Pakistani border was so rough that, because of the loud noise, it was impossible to understand a conversation *inside* Assaf's van. But no road that I bounced over or sloshed through was worse than the drive through the Salang Tunnel.

Driving southeast from Mazar back to Kabul was not easy. The cratered road, mountains, deep snow and, of course, the dangerous tunnel remained in place. We turned our escape into a clean two-day journey. We didn't leave before dawn as we had when traveling north from Kabul. Instead, we left at 2 p.m. on March 6, and stayed overnight at a guesthouse, where the food was plentiful and tasty, in Pul-i-Khumri, a city of 200,000 inhabitants. We attacked the Salang Tunnel the following morning. Gambling, we left Mirwiz, our teen-age mechanical wizard, behind.

Little time passed before I waved goodbye to the camel-brown and slate-gray steppes around Mazar. Ninety minutes from Mazar the air grew colder, and a broad valley glowed in green before we reached the base of mountains flecked with lime-green-colored earth and Georgia-like red clay. Snow topped the mountains. Below the snow, what looked like sheets of sliced stone stuck to the mountainsides as if glued in place to defy gravity. The mountains themselves, like giant stone trees, rose straight up on both sides of the road.

Conditions approaching the Salang Tunnel were as dangerous as when we headed north days earlier. Five small tunnels and roads rutted in snow and ice signaled the Salang ahead. Cars and trucks, too numerous to count under the circumstances, clogged the tunnel entrance. Large trucks were supposed to let cars pass into the tunnel first, but the trucks didn't wait and barged on. The tunnel was choked with water from melted snow, trapping cars in ponds. Too many vehicles were stuffed at the tunnel entrance, eager to run the gauntlet of avalanches and carbon monoxide. Drivers inside the tunnel shouted at others to turn off their engines, but most just shrugged and did nothing.

The scene was stunning on the other side of the Salang. A pristine wilderness circled by peak after peak of snow-covered mountains surrounded us, beauty ruined by the rusting hulks of war. The green, green grass of spring brought river valleys to life, though the road was no smoother.

We reached Kabul at 3:30 in the afternoon, more than twenty-five hours after leaving Mazar-ash-Sharif.

In the scrum to enter the tunnel the chain on our right rear tire snapped off. But we clanged on until Assaf could remove the chain outside the tunnel. Assaf didn't need Merwis.

After we cleared the tunnel, the van overheated. Assaf solved that problem easily and alone. He poured water into the radiator. I had learned that trick back in Millville, in 1958.

Salang Tunnel Entrance
MAXPPP / Alamy Stock Photo

The Blue Mosque, in Mazar-esh-Sharif, Afghanistan
Photo: Public Domain

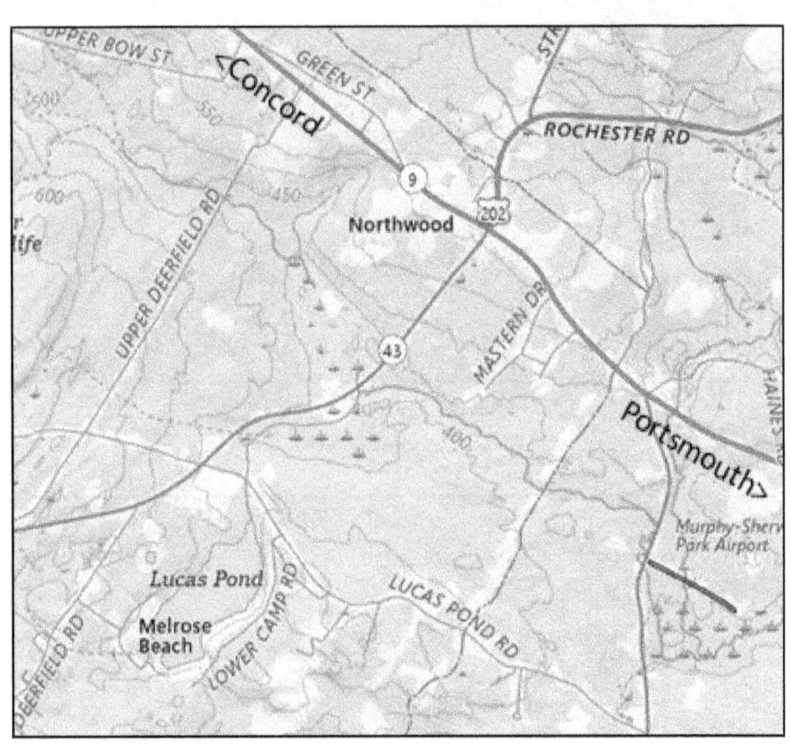
UPPER BOW ST
GREEN ST
<Concord
ROCHESTER RD
550
500
600
450
9
202
Northwood
UPPER DEERFIELD RD
MASTERN DR
43
400
Portsmouth>
Murphy-Sherv
Park Airport
Lucas Pond
LOWER CAMP RD
LUCAS POND RD
Melrose
Beach
DEERFIELD RD

13 | THE END OF THE ROAD

Not long ago, well within a contemporary lifetime, hitchhiking was routine. If I stood on a corner in my hometown, someone might stop and ask if I needed a lift. Often I did, although I wasn't hitching. Bumming a ride one day from Woonsocket, where I was born, to nearby Millville, where I was living, a vintage Porsche pulled over and I hopped in. Dempsey, a man I knew, was the driver. That eye-popping spin in a Fifties Porsche was my only hitch, anywhere, in a sports car.

Back in the Fifties and Sixties, male and mostly young people hitched to school, even to work or to an afternoon movie. Some hitched home on military leave. Many left their college dorms on weekends and hitched hundreds of miles to visit girlfriends or enjoy Mom's cooking, but mostly it was the girls who lured them. Hitching was often necessary, so quitting the verge wasn't considered. If fear rode along, it was never front lobe. Routine precautions and common sense were shields enough. A reaction to real or perceived dangers, fear would come later and thrust a dagger into the thumbs of later generations. The question then becomes: when was hitching no longer necessary or desirable? The answer is complex. All of a sudden, it seemed, there were too many cars on the road: old cars, new cars, clunkers that could still roll despite all kinds of ailments. Plus, too many people were driving. Even poor people had cars because they could afford them, and cars made life easier, if more expensive. Then came more highways and interstates, many of which banned hitching altogether. Fear also rode the asphalt, fear of just about everything that flowed from social disintegration and individual mistrust. Fear builds upon fear. A person who shows fear will get a reaction that exploits fear. Experience taught me that truism.

When hitching faded almost without notice into quaint stories of local lore and literature, the loss to society was as great as it was to individuals. Hitching, after all, was another way of learning about life and human nature and adapting, with unexpected and surprising flexibility, to life on the fly. Its loss represents gaps in trust that affect everyone and further weakens the thinning social commonwealth. The loss of hitchhiking as a means of transportation seems trivial on the American social landscape, where extreme and concentrated wealth and its pursuit are considered the premier liberal value. Its loss is anything but small or trivial; it added to the fragmentation among people. All those small losses, when added up, tear deeper into the fraying fabric of American society.

Hitching to college was my apprenticeship, the beginning of my time learning the art form. Bumming through deserts, over mountains, and across foreign cities, sharpened and polished the skills I learned routinely as a teenager. Meeting people I knew absolutely nothing about taught me to assess the unknown, to judge the honesty and authenticity of strangers, and to learn how to talk with them and figure out how they could help me. On far away dusty and desolate roads I learned that strangers talk more openly to strangers than they would to neighbors. It's easy to gossip and spread rumors to a stranger you'll never see again; easier, too, to speak truths. Sitting alone with a computer would have taught me other skills, but I would have learned zero about mastering the art of hitching and understanding its benefits. What I learned bumming rides couldn't have been learned if I drove my own car, unless I stopped for a hitchhiker.

The twenty first century, the year 2004 to be exact, seemed more than a century removed from 1958. Even the 1990s, when I reported from many of the world's great dungeons and lofts, seemed a hundred years distant from 2004. America's population was a mere 174,153,000 in 1958, when I thumbed my way to college and into the world. By 2004, the country's population had ballooned to 293,000,000. The disparity in the number of registered vehicles in the country was even greater between 1958 and 2004. In 1958, a mere 68,296,594 vehicles were registered from sea to shining sea, compared with 243,010,055 in 2004. So many more people and cars should have made it so much easier to thumb a ride, but that didn't happen.

Those statistics and personal experiences lead to the question of whether wealth and trust can ever co-exist.

OO

Crusted snow crackled beneath my boots. A bitter north wind whistled under my hood and into my right ear. A desire for garbanzo beans, tomatoes, lettuce, onions, cucumbers, and balsamic salad dressing urged me on. Not quite Little Red Riding Hood, I was headed through the leafless woods to a market three miles distant. Every three or four weeks for almost twelve months, I hit the road to replenish food supplies. This was a new century. It wasn't 1958, when I cursed motorists who seemed to thumb their noses at me, refusing to stop as I, whipped by the wind and water of their passing cars and semis, shivered under a highway bridge.

As I trudged through snow on the way to buy a few groceries, I was about one-hundred-and-twenty miles north of Millville. The moment was late January 2004, in the midst of a fierce winter. Cold as it was, life in Northwood, New Hampshire, wasn't like freezing in 2002, in a cinder block building in southeastern Afghanistan waiting for a blizzard to ease so I could pinpoint the Indian Ocean satellite and file a story. Life in Northwood was much more civilized.

Northwood is about half way between New Hampshire's short coast and its capital of Concord. Creativity was the reason for my seclusion: I was writing a book. My home was a small summer cottage, what I called a cabin, in the woods, at Lucas Pond. From early January until two weeks before turkey day, I wrestled with the coldest winter in generations, summer's nagging black flies, mosquitoes, sultry days, and autumn's panoply of hues. Alone, without a car or a television, I completed my writing mission.

During my sixty-fourth year, I also kept a daily journal about my writing life, spied trout at Lucas Pond, and eyed the fisher folk who tried to snag the unsuspecting rainbows for lunch. Hours spent thinking, writing, and walking through the woods offered time to meet a few folks who lived off the beaten path. I couldn't help but compare those acquaintances and neighbors to others I met in more desperate circumstances while roaming and reporting throughout the world.

Learning to push the right buttons and light a propane heater without blowing up the cabin was new to me. But it wasn't hardship training or learning to survive in Somalia. Flipping switches in the cabin's basement to make water flow in the winter of a deep freeze, and firing up the cabin's hot water heater without shouting for help was a different kind of test. But none of the above was anything like crawling around a minefield, one step behind amateur mine detectors in a land denuded by famine, drought and war.

From my perch in New Hampshire's woods, I was prepared to gaze at a bright new world, one filled with countless technological wonders and smarter people. A phone connection brought an Internet link to my computer while I walked miles for veggies and struggled to bring heat and hot water to the cabin. A native-American woman told me of experiences teaching the Inuit people in Alaska, and an Iraqi war veteran, another neighbor, talked of the difficulties of fighting in foreign lands, and the futility of war itself.

While individuals and societies crawl forward in unrelated circles, despite the havoc around them, other orbits never change. More than a quarter century from the Vietnam debacle and a little more than a decade from the first Persian Gulf War, America was invading again. In a short time, the triple threat team of George W. Bush, Richard Cheney, and Donald Rumsfeld invaded Afghanistan and followed that by invading Iraq. Elastic by nature of its history, land, and people, Afghanistan turned into the longest war in American history, that is if you don't count the conquest of a continent and of the North American natives who called it home. The invasion of Iraq was an error of immense consequences that remain to be fully realized.

The people of Northwood, New Hampshire were insulated from events in Afghanistan and Iraq. But they weren't insulated from changes in American society. They were so immersed in those changes that they were blind to them. The American nation became more diverse, and wicked old wounds slowly began to heal although reactionaries were close behind trying to scrape off the scabs. In galloping strides, kids were becoming expert at pushing buttons on devices that made their users seem like wizards. But those same kids were learning zero about how their government works or the history of how their country came to land where it was in the year 2004. Pushing buttons and punching keys came easily, but that expanding exercise made conversations more difficult, even impossible. More and more people, because of their ignorance, became more susceptible to lies and other forms of misinformation and disinformation, all of which came in massive amounts a few years later. Where reason and common sense should light the road ahead, rigid ideologues directed the populace into craters on the right side of the road, miles from the middle.

The young people who couldn't fathom what I was doing at Lucas Pond were only a few years ahead of their worsening time. Less than a decade after I worried about ignorance sweeping over the national landscape, Michele Bachmann strolled through the neighborhood, deep in a dense and manipulative fog all her own. Ignorance had landed right next door. A U.S. representative from Minnesota, Bachmann had her eye on the presidency: she wanted to be commander-in-chief of all the soldiers on land, pilots aloft, and all the sailors at sea. Her effects alone on the national treasury were awful to contemplate. A Republican and a leader of the right-wing reactionaries in Congress then called the Tea Party, she traveled to Concord,

New Hampshire's capital, fully armed for the big fight and all the ignorance it would take to win her party's nomination and, maybe, even the general election. In 2011, about thirty miles from the cabin in Northwood where I had lived seven years earlier, Bachmann tried to whiplash history. Neither caring nor knowing anything about history, she announced that the American Revolution began right there in New Hampshire's capital. Ah, forget about Lexington and Concord, Massachusetts, different towns in a different state where the farmers actually sent the Red Coats scurrying and bleeding back to Boston way back in the eighteenth century.

Bachmann's ignorance forced her to pull the plug on politics. She was ahead of her time, however, as the 2016 presidential election showed New Hampshire, the country, and the world. Shortly after Bachmann's electric rise and fall, Americans were fed from the highest podium a daily dose of lies to go with their daily bread. Lies, alternative, and false, facts, flowed from mouths to dictionaries.

My job was to live in the woods and write a book. Part of that life led me to walk for food. Once in a while I tried thumbing, bumming, hitching, just to see whether anyone would stop. I wanted to find out how much American society had changed since 1958, although I had a good idea of what rejection and mistrust would feel like. With gray hair showing under my hood and cap, I didn't get many rides. Was it age discrimination that kept me walking? Or was it fear of the unknown, a deep mistrust of anyone who lacked the means to own a car and, therefore, couldn't be trusted. Motorists had no war stories to tell. They didn't need me, a useless stranger, in their lives. And I didn't really need them. I could walk, go where I needed to go and get what I needed to get without help. If my thumb didn't work after twenty minutes or so on the verge, I walked.

Still, I learned, that a strange-looking geezer like me didn't lure strangers behind the wheel of a car or truck. Even when I wasn't hooded against below-zero temperatures and fiercely blowing snow, no one stopped. Nothing personal, I convinced myself, only generic and generational. A volunteer gave me a lift on one occasion because he wanted to see where I was living and whether I really was living where I said I was. He qualified as a natural and self-appointed detective, a protector of others who lived in the woods and distrusted strangers. He was, at least, unarmed and far removed from the secret police hovering in plain sight throughout the cities of the Middle East.

A couple of times, a fearless motorist stopped to give me a lift. What success I had came when I was hitching on Route 43 near Lucas Pond to the corner of Route 4, New Hampshire's original turnpike. Not once did I get a ride in the other direction, back to my cabin. That pattern continued throughout my writing year of 2004. After one particularly long day of trekking in the woods far down on Route 43, when I was tired and rain was beginning to dampen my curls, I needed a lift. Feeling hopeless I stuck out my thumb, got lucky before real lightning struck, and filled the straight flush. A relatively young man driving a small truck stopped. We talked briefly because there was little time for more, the drive to Route 4 being less than marathon distance. Quickly, the conversation turned to hitching being a dead art. New Hampshire's valleys, hills, and old mountains are a hiker's paradise, I said. Trying to have a little fun, I said the last time anyone was spotted hitching in the Granite State was in the summer of 1965, when a loner with a hunting rifle flung over his shoulder was spotted fleeing from the Great North Woods to the state's beaches, seeking a little sun on his neck. A grin crossed the driver's face; it was a sly smile, not wicked, and he didn't flinch.

"You know," he said, "we never know who we're picking up." We both laughed, but it was as if he knew what was coming next.

"Well," I said, my own sly smile shining, "I never know who's picking me up." We laughed again, louder this time, just before I said thanks, shut the door, and walked away from my last hitch.

ACKNOWLEDGMENTS

Larry Benedict and I met in 2012 while walking on a running track. In a wink, we got along. Larry and I started having lunch. Once a month, we ate a sandwich in downtown Portsmouth, New Hampshire, and occasionally in nearby Dover. Books were our main talking points, what we thought about our reading matter. Often we exchanged books. Larry talked little or not at all about his life at MIT, Johns Hopkins, and the University of Massachusetts, his alma mater. Every now and then, we'd discuss my reporting from other lands and the books I'd written about places where I truly was a foreigner. Sometimes, I'd mention my hitchhiking adventures and Larry would say, "You should write about those." Larry never insisted that I write those stories, but he seldom missed the opportunity to mention the prospect. Over time I took Larry's advice. This book is a result of Larry's belief in a good story. Thanks a million, Larry, for firing the starting gun.

Betsy Willeford and I have been friends and associates since 1978. For a decade, we worked together on The Miami (FL) News editorial page, winning numerous national awards along the way. Betsy inhales books, and never forgets the fine points. She's as good a book editor as any, and she edited my two previous books. After she read the manuscript for this book, Betsy said, "This is really good. You have to get this published." She insisted. At that point, I had no choice, except to thank Betsy for her help and motivation.

Judy Etheredge can spot a wayward comma, misplaced modifier or a typo of any sort from great distances. Rather than wait for

Judy to spot my errors after publication, I offered her a chance to save me from myself before the press rolled. Judy has done that well.

To many people -- historians and librarians, among others -- in Woonsocket, Rhode Island and Millville, Massachusetts, I owe gratitude that's impossible to measure. To the countless strangers who plucked me from desert trails, away from errant missiles, and through poisonous mountain tunnels, I owe treasure too large to repay.

I, among his large community of loyal book readers, owe a huge debt of gratitude to Tom Holbrook for keeping his RiverRun Bookstore and Piscataqua Press alive in the midst of stifling challenges to the book world.

www.ingramcontent.com/pod-product-compliance
Lightning Source LLC
Chambersburg PA
CBHW022129080426
42734CB00006B/289

9781958669303